Compact Guide to
North Carolina Carolina BIRDS

Curtis G. Smalling
Gregory Kennedy

LONE
PINE

Lone Pine Publishing International

© 2006 Lone Pine Publishing International Inc.
First printed in 2006   10 9 8 7 6 5 4 3 2 1
Printed in China

Distributed by Lone Pine Publishing
1808 B Street NW, Suite 140
Auburn, WA USA 98001

Website: www.lonepinepublishing.com

Library and Archives Canada Cataloguing in Publication

Smalling, Curtis G., 1963–

   Compact guide to North Carolina birds / Curtis G. Smalling, Gregory Kennedy.

Includes bibliographical references and index.
ISBN-13: 978-976-8200-03-7
ISBN-10: 976-8200-03-0

   1. Birds—North Carolina—Identification. 2. Bird watching—North Carolina.
I. Kennedy, Gregory, 1956– II. Title.

QL684.N8S63 2006   598'.09756   C2006-900000-X

Illustrations: Gary Ross, Ted Nordhagen, Ewa Pluciennik
Cover Illustration: Eastern Screech-Owl, by Gary Ross
Scanning & Digital Film: Elite Lithographers Co.
Egg Photography: Alan Bibby, Gary Whyte

PC: P13

Contents

WATERFOWL

Canada Goose
size 42 in • p. 18

Tundra Swan
size 54 in • p. 20

Wood Duck
size 17 in • p. 22

TURKEYS

Mallard
size 24 in • p. 24

Northern Pintail
size 27 in • p. 26

Wild Turkey
size 39 in • p. 28

DIVING BIRDS

Common Loon
size 31 in • p. 30

Pied-billed Grebe
size 13 in • p. 32

Cory's Shearwater
size 19 in • p. 34

Wilson's Storm-Petrel
size 7 in • p. 36

Northern Gannet
size 38 in • p. 38

Brown Pelican
size 48 in • p. 40

HERONS, IBISES & VULTURES

Double-crested Cormorant
size 29 in • p. 42

Great Blue Heron
size 51 in • p. 44

Great Egret
size 39 in • p. 46

Green Heron
size 18 in • p. 48

White Ibis
size 22 in • p. 50

Turkey Vulture
size 28 in • p. 52

Osprey
size 23 in • p. 54

Bald Eagle
size 36 in • p. 56

Sharp-shinned Hawk
size 12 in • p. 58

BIRDS OF PREY

Red-tailed Hawk
size 20 in • p. 60

American Kestrel
size 8 in • p. 62

Clapper Rail
size 14 in • p. 64

RAILS & COOTS

American Coot
size 14 in • p. 66

Black-bellied Plover
size 12 in • p. 68

Killdeer
size 10 in • p. 70

American Oystercatcher
size 18 in • p. 72

Spotted Sandpiper
size 7 in • p. 74

Sanderling
size 8 in • p. 76

SHOREBIRDS

Laughing Gull
size 16 in • p. 78

Herring Gull
size 24 in • p. 80

Royal Tern
size 20 in • p. 82

GULLS & ALLIES

Black Skimmer
size 18 in • p. 84

Rock Pigeon
size 12 in • p. 86

Mourning Dove
size 12 in • p. 88

DOVES & CUCKOOS

DOVES & CUCKOOS

OWLS

NIGHTJARS, SWIFTS & HUMMINGBIRDS

WOODPECKERS

FLYCATCHERS

VIREOS

JAYS & CROWS

Yellow-billed Cuckoo
size 12 in • p. 90

Eastern Screech-Owl
size 8 in • p. 92

Great Horned Owl
size 21 in • p. 94

Barred Owl
size 20 in • p. 96

Chuck-will's-widow
size 12 in • p. 98

Chimney Swift
size 5 in • p. 100

Ruby-throated Hummingbird
size 4 in • p. 102

Belted Kingfisher
size 12 in • p. 104

Red-bellied Woodpecker
size 10 in • p. 106

Downy Woodpecker
size 6 in • p. 108

Northern Flicker
size 12 in • p. 110

Pileated Woodpecker
size 16 in • p. 112

Acadian Flycatcher
size 6 in • p. 114

Great Crested Flycatcher
size 8 in • p. 116

Eastern Kingbird
size 9 in • p. 118

Red-eyed Vireo
size 6 in • p. 120

Blue Jay
size 11 in • p. 122

American Crow
size 19 in • p. 124

Purple Martin
size 7 in • p. 126

Barn Swallow
size 7 in • p. 128

Carolina Chickadee
size 5 in • p. 130

SWALLOWS

Tufted Titmouse
size 6 in • p. 132

White-breasted Nuthatch
size 6 in • p. 134

Carolina Wren
size 5 in • p. 136

CHICKADEES, NUTHATCHES & WRENS

Eastern Bluebird
size 7 in • p. 138

Wood Thrush
size 8 in • p. 140

American Robin
size 10 in • p. 142

BLUEBIRDS & THRUSHES

Gray Catbird
size 9 in • p. 144

Northern Mockingbird
size 10 in • p. 146

Brown Thrasher
size 11 in • p. 148

MIMICS & STARLINGS

European Starling
size 8 in • p. 150

Yellow-rumped Warbler
size 5 in • p. 152

Ovenbird
size 6 in • p. 154

WOOD-WARBLERS & TANAGERS

Common Yellowthroat
size 5 in • p. 156

Scarlet Tanager
size 7 in • p. 158

Eastern Towhee
size 8 in • p. 160

SPARROWS, GROSBEAKS & BUNTINGS

SPARROWS, GROSBEAKS & BUNTINGS

Song Sparrow
size 6 in • p. 162

White-throated Sparrow
size 7 in • p. 164

Dark-eyed Junco
size 6 in • p. 166

Northern Cardinal
size 8 in • p. 168

Rose-breasted Grosbeak
size 8 in • p. 170

Indigo Bunting
size 5 in • p. 172

BLACKBIRDS & ALLIES

Red-winged Blackbird
size 8 in • p. 174

Eastern Meadowlark
size 9 in • p. 176

Brown-headed Cowbird
size 7 in • p. 178

FINCHES

Orchard Oriole
size 6 in • p. 180

House Finch
size 5 in • p. 182

Introduction

If you have ever admired a songbird's pleasant notes, been fascinated by a soaring hawk or wondered how woodpeckers keep sawdust out of their nostrils, this book is for you. There is so much to discover about birds and their surroundings that birding is becoming one of the fastest growing hobbies on the planet. Many people find it relaxing, while others enjoy its outdoor appeal. Some people see it as a way to reconnect with nature, an opportunity to socialize with like-minded people or a way to monitor the environment.

Whether you are just beginning to take an interest in birds or can already identify many species, there is always more to learn. We've highlighted both the remarkable traits and the more typical behaviors displayed by some of our most abundant or noteworthy birds. A few live in specialized habitats, but most are common species that you have a good chance of encountering on most outings or in your backyard.

BIRDING IN NORTH CAROLINA

We are truly blessed by the geographical and biological diversity of North Carolina. In addition to supporting a wide range of breeding birds and year-round residents, our state hosts a large number of spring and fall migrants that move through our area on the way to their breeding and wintering grounds. In all, over 440 bird species have been seen and recorded in North Carolina.

Identifying birds in action and under varying conditions involves skill, timing and luck. The more you know about a bird—its range, preferred habitat, food preferences and hours and seasons of activity— the better your chances will be of seeing it. Generally, spring and

Sharp-shinned Hawk

fall are the busiest birding times. Temperatures are moderate then, many species of birds are on the move, and male songbirds are belting out their unique courtship songs. Birds are usually most active in the early morning hours, except in winter when they forage during the day when milder temperatures prevail.

Another useful clue for correctly recognizing birds is knowledge of their habitat. Simply put, a bird's habitat is the place where it normally lives. Some birds prefer open water, some are found in cattail marshes, others like mature coniferous forest and still other birds prefer abandoned agricultural fields overgrown with tall grass and shrubs. Habitats are just like neighborhoods: if you associate friends with the suburb in which they live, you can easily learn to associate specific birds with their preferred habitat. Only in migration, especially during inclement weather, do some birds leave their usual habitat.

North Carolina has a long tradition of friendly, recreational birding. In general, birders are willing to help beginners, share their knowledge and involve novices in their projects. Christmas bird counts, breeding bird surveys, nest box programs, migration monitoring and birding lectures and workshops provide a chance for birders of all levels to interact and share the splendor of birds. Bird hotlines provide up-to-date information on the sightings of rarities, which are often easier to relocate than you might think. For more information or to participate in these projects, contact the organizations listed on p. 11:

American Robin

The Carolina Bird Club
5009 Crown Point Lane
Wilmington, NC 28409
www.carolinabirdclub.org

Audubon North Carolina
123 Kingston Drive, Suite 206A
Chapel Hill, NC 27514
www.ncaudubon.org

North Carolina Birding Trail
NC Wildlife Resources Commission
1722 Mail Service Center
Raleigh, NC 27699-1722
www.ncbirdingtrail.org

NC Rare Bird Alert
(704) 733-2453

BIRD LISTING
Many birders list the species they have
seen during excursions or at home. It
is up to you to decide what kind of
list—systematic or casual—you
will keep, and you may choose
not to make lists at all. Lists may
prove rewarding in unexpected
ways, and after you visit a new
area, your list becomes a sou-
venir of your experiences there.
Keeping regular, accurate lists of
birds in your neighborhood can also
be useful for local researchers. It can
be interesting to compare the arrival
dates and last sightings of hummingbirds and other seasonal visitors, or to note the first sighting of
a new visitor to your area.

Red-tailed Hawk

BIRD FEEDING

Many people set up bird feeders in their backyard, especially in winter. It is possible to attract specific birds by choosing the right kind of food and style of feeder. Keep your feeder stocked through late spring, because birds have a hard time finding food before the flowers bloom, seeds develop and insects hatch. Contrary to popular opinion, birds do not become dependent on feeders, nor do they subsequently forget to forage naturally. Be sure to clean your feeder and the surrounding area regularly to prevent the spread of disease.

Landscaping your property with native plants is another way of providing natural food for birds. Flocks of waxwings have a keen eye for red mountain-ash berries and hummingbirds enjoy bee balm flowers. The cumulative effects of "nature-scaping" urban yards can be a significant step toward habitat conservation (especially when you consider that habitat is often lost in small amounts—a power line is cut in one area and a highway is built in another). Many good books and web sites about attracting wildlife to your backyard are available.

NEST BOXES

Another popular way to attract birds is to put up nest boxes, especially for House Wrens, Eastern Bluebirds, Tree Swallows and Purple Martins. Not all birds will use nest boxes: only species that normally use cavities in trees are comfortable in such confined spaces. Larger nest boxes can attract kestrels, owls and cavity-nesting ducks.

Purple Martin

ABOUT THE SPECIES ACCOUNTS

This book gives detailed accounts of 83 species of birds that can be expected in North Carolina on an annual basis. The order of the birds and their common and scientific names follow the American Ornithologists' Union's *Check-list of North American Birds* (7th edition, July 1998, and its supplements through 2005).

As well as showing the identifying features of the bird, each species account also attempts to bring the bird to life by describing its various character traits. One of the challenges of birding is that many species look different in spring and summer than they do in fall and winter. Many birds have breeding and nonbreeding plumages, and immature birds often look different from their parents. This book does not try to describe or illustrate all the different plumages of a species; instead, it tries to focus on the forms that are most likely to be seen in our area.

Red-winged Blackbird

ID: Large illustrations point out prominent field marks that will help you tell each bird apart. The descriptions favor easily understood language instead of technical terms. Some of the most common anatomical features of birds are pointed out in the Glossary illustration (p. 185).

Size: The average length of the bird's body from bill to tail, as well as wingspan, are given and are approximate measurements of the bird as it is seen in nature. The size is sometimes given as a range, because there is variation between individuals, or between males and females.

Voice: You will hear many birds, particularly songbirds, which may remain hidden from view. Memorable paraphrases of distinctive sounds will aid you in identifying a species by ear.

Status: A general comment, such as "common," "uncommon" or "rare," is usually sufficient to describe the relative abundance of a species. Situations are bound to vary somewhat since migratory pulses, seasonal changes and centers of activity tend to concentrate or disperse birds.

Habitat: The habitats listed describe where each species is most commonly found. Because of the freedom that flight gives them, birds can turn up in almost any type of habitat. However, they will usually be found in environments that provide the specific food, water, cover and, in some cases, nesting habitat that they need to survive.

Orchard Oriole

Similar Birds: Easily confused species are illustrated for each account. If you concentrate on the most relevant field marks, the subtle differences between species can be reduced to easily identifiable traits. Even experienced birders can mistake one species for another.

Nesting: In each species account, nest location and structure, clutch size, incubation period and parental duties are discussed. A photo of the bird's egg is also provided. Remember that birding ethics discourage the disturbance of active bird nests. If you disturb a nest, you may drive off the parents during a critical period or expose defenseless young to predators.

Range Maps: The range map for each species shows the overall range of the species in an average year. Most birds will confine their annual movements to this range, though each year some birds wander beyond their traditional boundaries. The maps show breeding, summer and winter ranges, as well as migratory pathways—areas of the region where birds may appear while en route to nesting or winter habitat. The representations of the pathways do not distinguish high-use migration corridors from areas that are seldom used.

Range Map Symbols

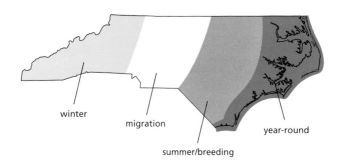

winter

migration

year-round

summer/breeding

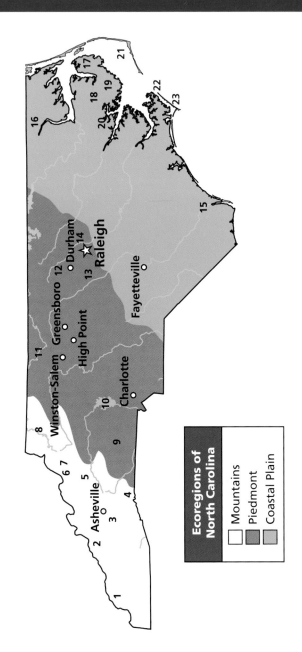

Ecoregions of
North Carolina

Mountains
Piedmont
Coastal Plain

TOP BIRDING SITES

From the barrier islands of Cape Hatteras to the breathtaking Blue Ridge Mountains, our state can be separated into three natural regions: the Mountains, the Piedmont and the Coastal Plain (with its associated shorelines). Each region is composed of a number of different habitats that support a wealth of wildlife.

There are hundreds of good birding areas throughout our region. The following areas have been selected to represent a broad range of bird communities and habitats, with an emphasis on accessibility.

1. Joyce Kilmer-Slickrock Wilderness Area
2. Great Smoky Mountains NP
3. Blue Ridge Parkway
4. Jackson Park
5. Mount Mitchell SP
6. Roan Mountain
7. Grandfather Mountain
8. New River SP
9. South Mountains SP
10. Lake Norman
11. Hanging Rock SP
12. Eno River SP
13. Jordan Lake SRA
14. Falls Lake SRA
15. Wilmington Area (Fort Fisher, Southport, Carolina Beach SP)
16. Merchants Millpond SP
17. Alligator River NWR
18. Pocosin Lakes NWR
19. Lake Mattamuskeet NWR
20. Goose Creek SP
21. Cape Hatteras National Seashore
22. Cedar Island NWR
23. Cape Lookout National Seashore

NP	- National Park
NWR	- National Wildlife Refuge
SP	- State Park
SRA	- State Recreation Area

Canada Goose

Branta canadensis

Thousands of Canada Geese used to descend on North Carolina each winter, but many birds now cut short their migration to enjoy the abundant food supply found in the corn and grain fields of the Midwest. Although a few migratory geese regularly visit our state each year, there are now many more resident nonmigratory birds. • The Canada Goose was split into two species in 2004. The larger subspecies are still known as Canada Geese, but the smaller subspecies have been renamed Cackling Geese. • Look for migrants, including Cackling Geese, at Lake Mattamuskeet NWR and Pocosin Lakes NWR; permanent residents can be found at public parks and golf courses.

Other ID: dark brown upperparts; light brown underparts. *In flight:* flocks fly in V-formation.
Size: *L* 3–4 ft; *W* up to 6 ft.
Voice: loud, familiar *ah-honk*.
Status: common permanent resident throughout North Carolina; migratory flocks over-winter in northeastern North Carolina.
Habitat: lakeshores, riverbanks, ponds, farmlands and city parks.

Similar Birds

Cackling Goose

Brant

long, black neck

white "chin strap"

short, black tail

white undertail coverts

Nesting: usually on the ground; female builds a nest of grass and mud, lined with down; white eggs are 3½ x 2¼ in; female incubates 3–8 eggs for 25–28 days; goslings are born in May.

Did You Know?

Canada Geese have been kept in captivity since the early 1800s, including a flock kept at Henderson by ornithologist John James Audubon.

Look For

Canada Geese will come in close for bread crumbs, but be aware that these large geese sometimes hiss and chase humans aggressively.

Tundra Swan
Cygnus columbianus

The magnificent Tundra Swan breeds in the Arctic and winters along the coast. This graceful bird is a long-lived species that mates for life. The young remain with their parents for their first winter in North Carolina, and then the family flies back to the breeding grounds together. • The eastern population of Tundra Swans is estimated at over 100,000 birds and is climbing steadily. These birds traditionally fed on aquatic plants, but in recent years have taken a liking to more widely available waste grain in agricultural areas. • Lake Mattamuskeet NWR and Pocosin Lakes NWR are good places to look for this swan.

Other ID: slightly concave bill; black feet.
Size: *L* 4–5 ft; *W* 6½ ft.
Voice: high-pitched, quivering *oo-oo-whoo* repeated in flight.
Status: common in winter.
Habitat: shallow areas of lakes and wetlands, agricultural fields and flooded pastures.

Similar Birds

Snow Goose

Mute Swan

yellow lores

neck is held straight up

Nesting: does not nest in North Carolina; nests in the Arctic; female builds a large nest mound lined with grass, feathers and down; creamy white eggs are $3\frac{1}{8}$ x 2 in; female incubates 4–7 eggs for 22–25 days.

Did You Know?

Tundra Swans take over three months to migrate from the Atlantic Coast to the Arctic, but they spend only about 120 hours in the air.

Look For

Tundra Swans and egrets are our only birds with completely white plumage. White Ibises, Snow Geese, Northern Gannets and American White Pelicans have black wing tips.

Wood Duck

Aix sponsa

Like their name implies, beautiful Wood Ducks are forest-dwelling ducks, equipped with fairly sharp claws for perching on branches and nesting in tree cavities. Shortly after hatching, brave ducklings often jump 20 feet or more out of their nest cavities. Like downy ping-pong balls, they bounce off the ground on landing and are seldom injured. • If Wood Ducks nest in a local park or farmyard, do not approach the nest, because fewer disturbances increase the young's chance of survival.

Other ID: *Male:* glossy, green head with some white streaks; white-spotted, purplish chestnut breast; dark back and hindquarters. *Female:* gray-brown upperparts; white belly.
Size: *L* 15–20 in; *W* 30 in.
Voice: *Male:* ascending *ter-wee-wee. Female:* squeaky *woo-e-e-k.*
Status: fairly common across the state as a breeder, becoming scarce in the mountains in winter.
Habitat: swamps, ponds, marshes and lakeshores with wooded edges.

Similar Birds

Hooded Merganser

Look For

Thousands of nest boxes erected across the Wood Duck's breeding range and hunting restrictions have helped Wood Ducks recover from near extinction.

white, teardrop-shaped eye patch

crest slicked back from crown

black and white shoulder slash

mottled brown breast streaked with white

golden sides

white "chin" and throat

Nesting: in a hollow, tree cavity or artificial nest box; usually near water; cavity is lined with down; white to buff eggs are 2⅛ x 1⅝ in; female incubates 9–14 eggs for 25–35 days.

Did You Know?

Female Wood Ducks often return to the same nest site year after year, especially after successfully raising a brood. The young's chance of survival may increase at traditional nest sites, where the adults are familiar with potential threats.

Mallard
Anas platyrhynchos

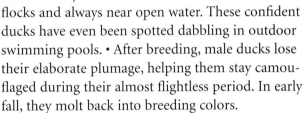

The male Mallard, with his shiny green head and chestnut brown breast, is the classic wild duck. Mallards can be seen year-round, often in flocks and always near open water. These confident ducks have even been spotted dabbling in outdoor swimming pools. • After breeding, male ducks lose their elaborate plumage, helping them stay camouflaged during their almost flightless period. In early fall, they molt back into breeding colors.

Other ID: orange feet. *Male:* white "necklace"; black tail feathers curl upward. *Female:* mottled brown overall. *In flight:* dark blue speculum bordered by white.
Size: *L* 20–28 in; *W* 3 ft.
Voice: quacks; female's call is louder and longer than male's.
Status: common permanent resident across the state.
Habitat: lakes, wetlands, rivers, city parks, agricultural areas and sewage lagoons, especially freshwater lakes and ponds in the Coastal Plain in winter.

Similar Birds

Northern Shoveler

American Black Duck

Common Merganser

glossy, green head

yellow bill

dark blue speculum
bordered by white

♂

♀

orange bill
spattered
with black

Nesting: female builds a grass nest on the
ground or under a bush; creamy, grayish or
greenish white eggs are 2¼ × 1⅝ in; female
incubates 7–10 eggs for 26–30 days.

Did You Know?

A brooding hen's body
heat is enough to increase
the growth rate of nearby
grasses, which she then
manipulates to further
conceal her nest.

Look For

Mallards readily hybridize
with a variety of other duck
species, often producing offspring with very peculiar
plumages.

Northern Pintail
Anas acuta

Its long neck and long, tapered tail put this dabbling duck in a class of its own. Sadly, thousands of pintails are killed annually because they mistake lead shotgun pellets or fishing sinkers for the hard grains and seeds that they regularly eat. There is enough lead in a single ingested pellet to poison a bird. Lead-free alternatives are becoming readily available, and several proactive states have placed bans or restrictions on lead sinkers. • Good places to look for it are Lake Mattamuskeet NWR, Pea Island NWR and Pocosin Lakes NWR.

Other ID: long, slender neck; dark, glossy bill. *Male:* dusty gray body plumage; black and white hindquarters. *Female:* mottled, light brown overall.
Size: *Male:* L 25–30 in; W 34 in. *Female:* L 20–22 in; W 34 in.
Voice: *Male:* soft, whistling call. *Female:* rough quack.
Status: common winter resident in northeast North Carolina; fairly common farther south in the Coastal Plain; uncommon to rare migrant inland.
Habitat: shallow wetlands, flooded fields and lake edges.

Similar Birds

Mallard (p. 24)

Gadwall

Blue-winged Teal

chocolate
brown head

♂

♀

white on breast
extends up sides
of neck

♂

♀

long, tapering
tail feathers

Nesting: does not nest in North Carolina; nests in the north-central U.S. and in Canada; in a small depression in vegetation; nest of grass, leaves and moss is lined with down; greenish buff eggs are 2⅛ x 1½ in; female incubates 6–12 eggs for 22–25 days.

Did You Know?

The Northern Pintail, one of the most abundant waterfowl species on the continent, migrates at night at altitudes of up to 3000 ft.

Look For

The long, pointed tail of the male Northern Pintail is easily seen in flight and points skyward when the bird tips up to dabble.

Wild Turkey
Meleagris gallopavo

If Congress had taken Benjamin Franklin's advice in 1782, our national emblem would be the Wild Turkey instead of the majestic Bald Eagle. • This charismatic bird is the only native North American animal that has been widely domesticated. • Early in life both male and female turkeys gobble. The females eventually outgrow this practice, leaving males to gobble competitively for the honor of mating. • Turkeys can be seen at Grandfather Mountain, Elk Knob SNA, Hanging Rock SP and along the Blue Ridge Parkway.

Other ID: dark, glossy, iridescent body plumage. *Male:* colorful head and body; red wattles; black-tipped breast feathers. *Female:* smaller; blue-gray head; brown-tipped breast feathers.
Size: *Male: L* 3–3½ ft; *W* 5½ ft. *Female: L* 3 ft; *W* 4 ft.
Voice: wide array of sounds; courting male gobbles loudly.
Status: common permanent resident in the mountains and Piedmont; fairly common in most Coastal Plain counties.
Habitat: deciduous, mixed and riparian woodlands; occasionally eats waste grain and corn in late fall and winter.

Similar Birds

Ring-necked Pheasant

Look For

Eastern Wild Turkeys have brown or rusty tail tips and are slimmer than domestic turkeys, which have white tail tips.

naked, blue-red head

barred, copper-colored tail

♂

long, central breast tassle

Nesting: under thick cover in a woodland or at a field edge; nests in a depression on ground, lined with vegetation; brown-speckled, pale buff eggs are 2½ x 1¾ in; female incubates 10–12 eggs for up to 28 days.

Did You Know?

The Wild Turkey was once very common throughout most of eastern North America, but during the early 20th century, habitat loss and overhunting took a toll on this bird. Today, efforts at restoration have reestablished the Wild Turkey nearly statewide.

Common Loon
Gavia immer

Common Loons are well suited to their aquatic lifestyle. These divers have nearly solid bones that make them less buoyant (most birds have hollow bones), and their feet are placed well back on their bodies for underwater propulsion. Small bass, perch and sunfish are all fair game for these excellent underwater hunters. • A loon's heavy body and relatively small wing size means it requires a lengthy sprint over water before taking off. • Look for these divers nearshore in winter up and down the coast and in Pamlico Sound and the Fort Fisher area.

Other ID: *Breeding:* black and white checkerboard upperparts; white necklace; green-black head; white breast and underparts. *In flight:* long wings beat constantly; legs trail behind tail.
Size: *L* 28–35 in; *W* 4 ft.
Voice: generally silent in winter; alarm call is a quavering tremolo.
Status: common winter resident in ocean and large brackish waters; fairly common migrant at inland lakes across the state.
Habitat: ocean, brackish sounds and lakes and ponds.

Similar Birds

Red-throated Loon

Red-breasted
Merganser

Double-crested
Cormorant

hunchback appearance

nonbreeding

stout, thick black bill

sandy, brown back

light underparts

nonbreeding

Nesting: does not nest in North Carolina; nests in Great Lakes region and in Canada; nest is a mound of aquatic vegetation; darkly spotted, olive brown eggs are 3½ x 2¼ in; pair incubates 1–3 eggs for 24–31 days.

Did You Know?

Hungry loons will chase fish to depths of 180 ft— as deep as an Olympic-sized swimming pool is long.

Look For

Rear-placed legs make walking on land awkward for these birds. The word "loon" is probably derived from the Scandinavian word *lom*, which means "clumsy person."

Pied-billed Grebe
Podilymbus podiceps

Relatively solid bones and the ability to partially deflate their air sacs allow Pied-billed Grebes to sink below the water's surface like tiny submarines. These birds tend to stick to the shallow waters of quiet marshes, lakes and ponds where they can disappear into the cattails without leaving a trace. • Pied-billed Grebes are year-round residents in North Carolina, but they are most common from September to May when solitary individuals are often seen on larger rivers and lakes near the coast.

Other ID: *Breeding:* all-brown body; black ring on pale bill; black throat; pale belly; pale eye ring. *Nonbreeding:* yellow bill lacks black ring.
Size: *L* 12–15 in; *W* 16 in.
Voice: not often heard; loud, whooping call begins quickly, then slows down: *kuk-kuk-kuk cow cow cow cowp cowp cowp.*
Status: common in migration; common (except in higher mountains) winter resident; rare breeder.
Habitat: *Breeding:* coast or occasionally inland. *In migration* and *winter:* freshwater areas with impoundments or marshes.

Similar Birds

American Coot
(p. 66)

Red-necked Grebe

Horned Grebe

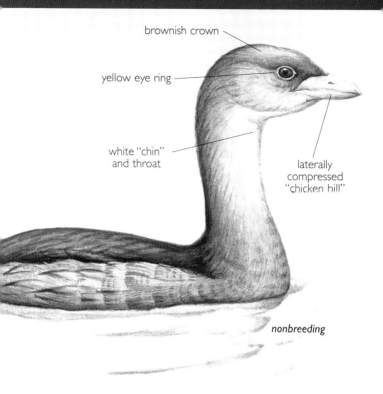

brownish crown

yellow eye ring

white "chin" and throat

laterally compressed "chicken bill"

nonbreeding

Nesting: in wetlands; floating platform nest of decaying plants is anchored to emergent vegetation; white to buff eggs are 1⅝ × 1¼ in; pair incubates 4–5 eggs for about 23 days and raises the striped young together.

Did You Know?

When frightened by an intruder, these grebes cover their eggs and slide underwater, leaving a nest that looks like nothing more than a mat of debris.

Look For

Dark plumage, individually webbed toes and a chicken-like bill distinguish the Pied-billed Grebe from other waterfowl.

Cory's Shearwater
Calonectris diomedea

The Cory's Shearwater nests half a world away on the rocky cliffs of Mediterranean islands. After breeding, it disperses thousands of miles to the East Coast of the U.S. or to the Indian Ocean, making it the only shearwater that both breeds and overwinters in the Northern Hemisphere.
• This stalwart shearwater was first spotted off the coast of New England in 1880 by Charles Barney Cory. • To best see this bird, you should take a pelagic trip (or fishing charter) out of Cape Hatteras or the Wilmington area.

Other ID: dark wing tips and tail tip. *In flight:* wings slightly bent while gliding; clean white underwings.
Size: L 18–21 in; W 3¾ ft.
Voice: usually silent at sea; occasionally utters a hoarse, nasal cry.
Status: common summer offshore resident.
Habitat: open ocean; favors warm waters; flocks gather near food sources.

Similar Birds

Greater Shearwater

Audubon's Shearwater

Black-capped Petrel

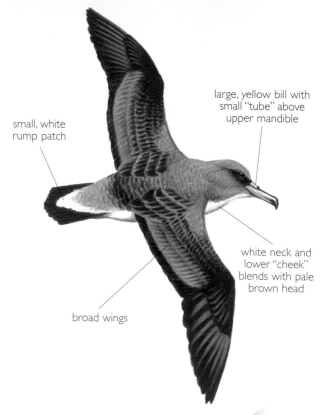

large, yellow bill with small "tube" above upper mandible

small, white rump patch

white neck and lower "cheek" blends with pale brown head

broad wings

Nesting: does not nest in North Carolina; nests on islands in the Mediterranean Sea; colonial nester; digs a nesting tunnel into rocks; visits colony only at night; dull white egg is 2½ x 1¾ in; pair incubates 1 egg for 52–56 days.

Did You Know?

Diomedea is a form of the name Diomedes, for a Trojan War hero whose companions were turned into birds when their ship was lost at sea.

Look For

Before breeding at age seven, young shearwaters may spend years soaring over the open ocean without ever touching down on land.

Wilson's Storm-Petrel
Oceanites oceanicus

The Wilson's Storm-Petrel is a long-distance migrant that travels from its Antarctic nesting grounds to the edge of the Arctic and back again each year. This long-legged storm-petrel flies with an arcing, roller coaster–like flight pattern. • While foraging at the outer portion of the continental shelf, the Wilson's Storm-Petrel may hover, pattering its feet on the water's surface to stir up small shrimp, crustaceans and fish. It also follows fishing boats to steal an easy meal. • This bird is best seen on pelagic trips (or fishing charters) out of Cape Hatteras or the Wilmington area.

Other ID: *In flight:* shallow, stiff wingbeats, suggesting a swallow.
Size: L 7 in; W 18 in.
Voice: usually silent; soft peeping or chattering may be heard from groups of feeding birds.
Status: common offshore summer visitor.
Habitat: open ocean, especially over the continental shelf; occasionally wanders close to land along the coast.

Similar Birds

Leach's Storm-Petrel

Greater Shearwater

Sooty Shearwater

pale patch on underwings

very dark brown overall

white rump and undertail coverts

square tail may appear notched

toes extend beyond end of tail

Nesting: does not nest in North Carolina; nests on isolated islands in the Antarctic region; colony nester; male digs a burrow, usually under rocks; nest chamber is lined with vegetation; white egg is 1 1/4 x 1 in; pair incubates 1 egg for 39–48 days.

Did You Know?

Storm-petrels can live more than 20 years. The oldest known of these birds, a Leach's Storm-Petrel, lived to be 36.

Look For

Watch for these birds off our coast between mid-May and mid-October, during winter in the Southern Hemisphere.

Northern Gannet
Morus bassanus

The Northern Gannet, with its elegant face "mask" and high forehead, slices through the open ocean air with blackened wing tips. • This gentle-looking bird does not breed until it is at least five years of age, and it mates for life. To reestablish their bond each year, pairs affectionately dip their bills to the breast of their mate, bow, raise their wings and preen each other. • Squadrons of gannets soaring at heights of more than 100 feet above the water will suddenly stop their flight by folding their wings back and simultaneously plunge headfirst into the ocean depths in pursuit of schooling fish.

Other ID: *In flight:* black wing tips; long, narrow wings; pointed tail; black feet. *Immature:* variably mottled with brown and gray.
Size: L 3–3¼ ft; W 6 ft.
Voice: usually silent at sea; feeding flocks may exchange grating growls.
Status: common over open ocean; nearshore in winter and migration from November to May; occasionally seen in larger brackish sounds.
Habitat: roosts and feeds in open ocean waters most of the year; often seen well offshore; regularly seen inshore during migration.

Similar Birds

Snow Goose

Look For

Immature gannets have white uppertail coverts, but otherwise resemble boobies because of their mottled plumage and dark underwings.

immature

thick, tapered, pale gray bill

buffy wash on nape

black wing tips

Nesting: does not nest in North Carolina; nests on islands in the Canadian Atlantic; in a shallow hollow on a mound of material, usually seaweed, lined with feathers and other plants; dull, chalky white egg is 3¼ x 2 in; pair incubates 1 egg (rarely 2) for 43–45 days.

Did You Know?

Gannets have air sacs under their skin that can be inflated to help cushion the impact of aerial dives into the ocean.

Brown Pelican
Pelecanus occidentalis

With even wingbeats, Brown Pelicans float gracefully above the sunbathers and fishing boats along North Carolina's coastline. These conspicuous waterbirds perch on beaches, rocks and pilings or course the troughs in single file. • In the 1950s and 1960s, DDT-related reproductive failures caused Brown Pelicans to nearly disappear in North Carolina and in many areas of the southeastern U.S. Since these highly persistent pesticides were banned in the 1970s, pelican populations have recovered. • Brown Pelicans can be seen anywhere along the coast, and there is a large breeding colony near Wilmington.

Other ID: *Nonbreeding:* white neck; head washed with yellow; pale yellowish pouch.
Size: L 4 ft; W 7 ft.
Voice: generally silent.
Status: common permanent resident; species of special concern.
Habitat: coastal and estuarine waters, ranging over the continental shelf in some areas; visits offshore islands; roosts on protected islets, sandbars and piers.

Similar Birds

American White
Pelican

Look For

Brown Pelicans are strictly a coastal species, seldom encountered away from marine or intertidal habitats.

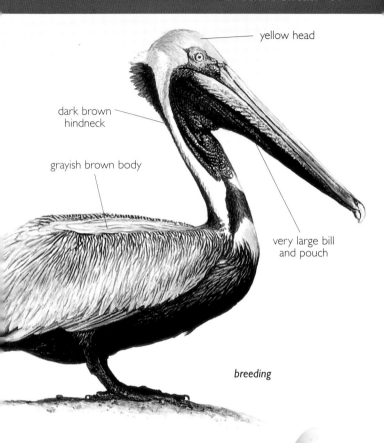

yellow head

dark brown
hindneck

grayish brown body

very large bill
and pouch

breeding

Nesting: nests on ground; scrape nest or an
elaborate platform of sticks; chalky white eggs are
3 x 2 in; pair incubates 2–3 eggs under footwebs
for 29–32 days.

Did You Know?

The Brown Pelican forages by a unique plunge-dive method:
while in flight, it folds its wings, pulls back its head and dives
headfirst into the water. Only the Brown Pelican forages this
way—other pelican species scoop up their prey.

Double-crested Cormorant

Phalacrocorax auritus

The Double-crested Cormorant looks like a bird but smells and swims like a fish. With a long, rudderlike tail and excellent underwater vision, this slick-feathered bird has mastered the underwater world. Most waterbirds have waterproof feathers, but the Double-crested Cormorant's feather structure allows water in. "Wettable" feathers make this bird less buoyant, which in turn makes it a better diver. • Look for huge cormorant flocks on dredge material islands easily seen from any of the coastal ferries.

Other ID: all-black body; blue eyes. *Immature:* brown upperparts; buff throat and breast; yellowish throat patch. *In flight:* rapid wingbeats; kinked neck.
Size: L 26–32 in; W 4¼ ft.
Voice: generally quiet; may issue piglike grunts or croaks, especially near nest colonies.
Status: common along the coast year-round; increasingly common as an inland migrant all the way to mountains.
Habitat: large lakes and large, meandering rivers.

Similar Birds

Anhinga

Common Loon
(p. 30)

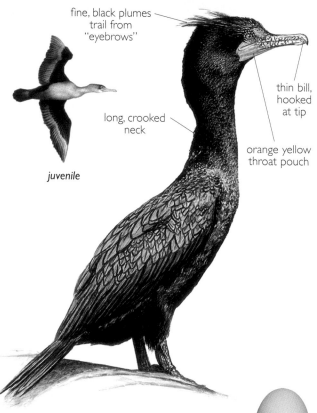

fine, black plumes trail from "eyebrows"

thin bill, hooked at tip

long, crooked neck

orange yellow throat pouch

juvenile

Nesting: colonial; on an island or high in a tree; platform nest is made of sticks and guano; pale blue eggs are 2 x 1½ in; pair incubates 2–7 eggs for 25–30 days.

Did You Know?

Japanese fishermen sometimes use cormorants on leashes to catch fish. This traditional method of fishing is called *Ukai*.

Look For

Double-crested Cormorants often perch on trees or piers with their wings partially spread to dry their feathers and regulate body temperature.

Great Blue Heron
Ardea herodias

The long-legged Great Blue Heron has a stealthy, often motionless hunting strategy. It waits for a fish or frog to approach, spears the prey with its bill, then flips its catch into the air and swallows the prey whole. Herons usually hunt near water, but they also stalk fields and meadows in search of rodents. • Great Blue Herons settle in communal treetop nests called rookeries. Nesting herons are sensitive to human disturbance, so observe this bird's behavior from a distance.

Other ID: blue-gray overall; long, dark legs. *Breeding:* richer colors; plumes streak from crown and throat. *In flight:* black upperwing tips; legs trail behind body; slow, steady wingbeats.
Size: L 4¼–4½ ft; W 6 ft.
Voice: quiet away from the nest; occasional harsh *frahnk frahnk frahnk* during takeoff.
Status: common permanent resident; most common in the Coastal Plain, especially in winter; breeds in all parts of the state but uncommon as breeder in the mountain region.
Habitat: forages along edges of rivers, lakes and marshes; also in fields and wet meadows.

Similar Birds

Little Blue Heron

Black-crowned Night-Heron

neck folds back over shoulders

black plumes above eye

straight, yellow bill

long, curving neck with black markings on throat

chestnut brown thighs

Nesting: colonial; adds to stick platform nest over years; nest width can reach 4 ft; pale bluish green eggs are 2½ x 1¾ in; pair incubates 4–7 eggs for approximately 28 days.

Did You Know?

The Great Blue Heron is the tallest of all herons and egrets in North America.

Look For

In flight, the Great Blue Heron folds its neck back over its shoulders in an S-shape. Similar-looking cranes stretch their necks out when flying.

Great Egret
Ardea alba

The plumes of Great Egrets and Snowy Egrets
(Egretta thula) were widely used to decorate hats in
the early 20th century. An ounce of egret feathers
cost as much as $32—more than an ounce of gold
at that time—and, as a result, egret populations
began to disappear. Some of the first conservation
legislation in North America was enacted to outlaw
the hunting of Great Egrets. We recently celebrated
the 100th anniversary of Teddy Roosevelt's estab-
lishment, in 1903, of the nation's first national
wildlife refuge, Pelican Island, Florida. • These
beautiful birds can be found at Lake Mattamuskeet
NWR, Pea Island NWR and the Fort Fisher area.

Other ID: all-white plumage. *In flight:* neck folds
back over shoulders; legs extend backward.
Size: L 3–3½ ft; W 4 ft.
Voice: rapid, low-pitched, loud *cuk-cuk-cuk.*
Status: common at the coast as a permanent resident; fairly common as an inland migrant, especially
in late summer at lakes and river systems in the
mountains and Piedmont.
Habitat: marshes, open riverbanks, irrigation canals and
lakeshores.

Similar Birds

Snowy Egret

Cattle Egret

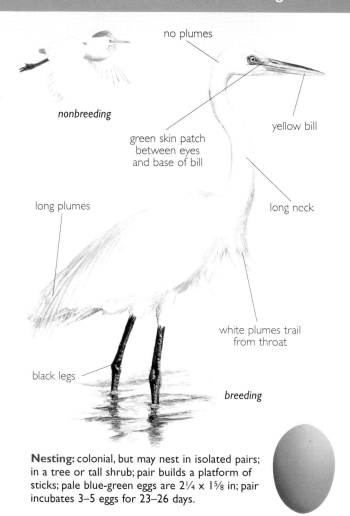

nonbreeding

no plumes

yellow bill

green skin patch
between eyes
and base of bill

long neck

long plumes

white plumes trail
from throat

black legs

breeding

Nesting: colonial, but may nest in isolated pairs; in a tree or tall shrub; pair builds a platform of sticks; pale blue-green eggs are 2¼ × 1⅝ in; pair incubates 3–5 eggs for 23–26 days.

Did You Know?

The Great Egret is the symbol for the National Audubon Society, one of the oldest conservation organizations in the United States.

Look For

Great Egrets are named for their impressive breeding plumes, or "aigrettes," which can grow up to 4½ ft long!

Green Heron
Butorides virescens

This crow-sized heron sits hunched on a shaded branch at the water's edge as it stalks frogs and small fish lurking in the weedy shallows, stabbing prey with its bill. • Some of this heron's habitat has been lost to wetland drainage or channelization in the southern states, but the building of farm ponds or reservoirs has created habitat in other areas. • Look for Green Herons at Alligator River NWR, Pea Island NWR and other coastal freshwater marshes.

Other ID: stocky body; relatively short, yellow-green legs; long bill is dark above and greenish below; short tail. *Breeding male:* bright orange legs.
Size: *L* 15–22 in; *W* 26 in.
Voice: generally silent; alarm and flight call are a loud *kowp, kyow* or *skow.*
Status: fairly common across the mountains and Piedmont as a breeder; abundant in the Coastal Plain in summer and migration periods; uncommon in winter at freshwater coastal swamps and marshes in the southern section.
Habitat: swamps, marshes, lakes and streams with dense shoreline or emergent vegetation.

Similar Birds

Black-crowned
Night-Heron

Least Bittern

American Bittern

dark,
iridescent back

green-black
crown

chestnut face
and neck

Nesting: nests singly or in small, loose groups; stick platform in a tree or shrub, usually close to water; blue-green to green eggs are 1½ x 1⅛ in; pair incubates 3–5 eggs for 19–21 days.

Did You Know?

Green Herons have been seen baiting fish to the surface by dropping small bits of debris such as twigs, vegetation or feathers on the water.

Look For

The scientific name *virescens* is Latin for "growing or becoming green" and refers to this bird's transition from a streaky brown juvenile to a greenish adult.

White Ibis
Eudocimus albus

White Ibises congregate on our coastline, often close to heronries, picking slowly through the mud for tasty crabs or crayfish. These birds can be cunning thieves, stealing food from other wading birds and, if the opportunity arises, even snatching nest-building material from others in their own colony.
• Breeding success is heavily dependent on the rainy season of late April or May when freshwater pools form, a necessity for feeding the salt-sensitive young. • This bird can be found at Battery Island Audubon North Carolina Sanctuary in the Southport area.

Other ID: *Immature:* brown-gray head, neck and upperparts; white rump and belly. *In flight:* small, dark wing tips; outstretched neck.
Size: *L* 22 in; *W* 3 ft.
Voice: mostly silent; throaty alarm or flight call: *hungk-hungk-hungk.*
Status: common permanent resident at the coast; more common southward; uncommon migrant inland.
Habitat: shallow water, estuaries, flooded fields and swamps.

Similar Birds

Glossy Ibis

Long-billed Curlew

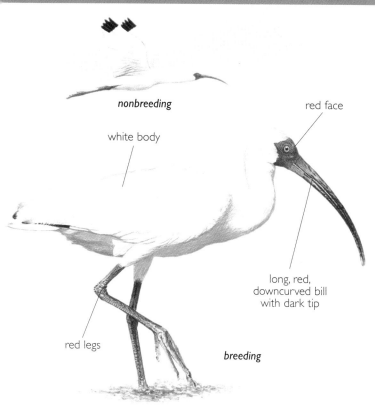

nonbreeding

white body

red face

long, red,
downcurved bill
with dark tip

red legs

breeding

Nesting: colonial; barrier islands, dredge material islands or forested swamps; nest is a platform of sticks or reeds; brown-splotched, pale buff eggs are 2¼ x 1⅝ in; pair incubates 2–4 eggs for 21–22 days.

Did You Know?

A Great Egret sometimes forages next to a White Ibis, snatching food that the ibis scares to the surface but cannot reach.

Look For

These highly nomadic birds commute for miles between nesting and feeding areas in long, cohesive lines or "V" patterns that may be a mile long.

Turkey Vulture

Cathartes aura

Turkey Vultures are intelligent, playful and social birds. Groups live and sleep together in large trees, or roosts. Some roost sites are over a century old and have been used by the same family of vultures for several generations. • A vulture's bill and feet are much less powerful than those of eagles, hawks or falcons, which kill live prey. Its red, featherless head may appear grotesque, but this adaptation allows the bird to stay relatively clean while feeding on messy carcasses. • Look for Turkey Vultures at coastal sites in winter, including Alligator River NWR and Mattamuskeet NWR, as well as along the Blue Ridge Parkway during migration.

Other ID: *Immature:* gray head. *In flight:* head appears small; wings are held in a shallow "V"; rocks from side to side when soaring.
Size: *L* 25–31 in; *W* 5½–6 ft.
Voice: generally silent; occasionally produces a hiss or grunt if threatened.
Status: common permanent resident statewide, becoming scarce at higher elevations in winter.
Habitat: usually flies over open country, shorelines or roads; rarely over forests.

Similar Birds

Black Vulture

Golden Eagle

Bald Eagle
(p. 56)

silver gray flight
feathers

bare, red head

brownish black
overall

pale, hooked bill

Nesting: in a cave, crevice, log or among boulders; uses no nest material; dull white eggs are 2¾ x 2 in; pair incubates 2 eggs for up to 41 days.

Did You Know?

A threatened Turkey Vulture will play dead or throw up. The odor of its vomit repulses attackers, much like the odor of a skunk's spray.

Look For

No other bird uses updrafts and thermals in flight as well as the Turkey Vulture. Pilots have reported seeing vultures soaring at 20,000 ft.

Osprey
Pandion haliaetus

The Osprey is almost always found near water. While hunting for fish, this bird hovers in the air before hurling itself in a dramatic headfirst dive. An instant before striking the water, it rights itself and thrusts its feet forward to grasp its quarry. The Osprey has specialized feet for gripping slippery prey—two toes point forward, two point backward and all are covered with sharp spines. • The Osprey is one of the most widely distributed birds in the world—it is found on every continent except Antarctica. • Ospreys can be found at Pea Island NWR, Mattamuskeet NWR and the Southport area.

Other ID: yellow eyes; pale crown. *Male:* all-white throat. *Female:* fine, dark "necklace." *In flight:* long wings are held in a shallow "M"; dark "wrist" patches; brown and white tail bands.
Size: *L* 22–25 in; *W* 5½–6 ft.
Voice: series of melodious ascending whistles: *chewk-chewk-chewk;* also a familiar *kip-kip-kip.*
Status: common nester on the coast; common migrant statewide; uncommon on the coast in winter.
Habitat: lakes and slow-flowing rivers and streams; estuaries and bays in migration.

Similar Birds

Bald Eagle (p. 56)

Rough-legged Hawk

dark eye line

gray bill

♂

long wings
extend past tail

♂

gray feet

Nesting: on a treetop or artificial structure, usually near water; massive stick nest is reused annually; yellowish, brown-blotched eggs are 2⅜ x 1¾ in; pair incubates 2–4 eggs for 38 days.

Did You Know?

The Osprey's dark eye line blocks the glare of the sun on the water, enabling the bird to spot fish near the water's surface.

Look For

Ospreys build bulky nests on high, artificial structures such as communication towers and utility poles, or on buoys and channel markers over water.

Bald Eagle

Haliaeetus leucocephalus

This majestic sea eagle hunts mostly fish and is often found near water. While soaring hundreds of feet high in the air, an eagle can spot fish swimming underwater and small rodents scurrying through the grass. Eagles also scavenge carrion and steal food from other birds. • Bald Eagles do not mature until their fourth or fifth year—only then do they develop the characteristic white head and tail plumage. • Look for Bald Eagles at Jordan Reservoir, Falls Lake and Mattamuskeet NWR.

Other ID: *1st year:* dark overall; dark bill; some white in underwings. *2nd year:* dark "bib"; white in underwings. *3rd year:* mostly white plumage; yellow eyes. *4th year:* light head with dark facial streak; variable pale and dark plumage; yellow bill.
Size: *L* 30–43 in; *W* 5½–8 ft.
Voice: thin, weak squeal or gull-like cackle: *kleek-kik-kik-kik* or *kah-kah-kah.*
Status: fairly common winter resident in the northeastern Coastal Plain and large inland lakes; uncommon breeder in the Piedmont and coastal sections; uncommon migrant in mountains.
Habitat: seacoasts, estuaries, large lakes and rivers.

Similar Birds

Golden Eagle

Osprey (p. 54)

white head and tail

yellow bill

yellow feet

Nesting: in a tree; usually, but not always, near water; huge stick nest is often reused for many years; white eggs are 2¾ x 2⅛ in; pair incubates 1–3 eggs for 34–36 days.

Did You Know?

The Bald Eagle, a symbol of freedom, longevity and strength, became the emblem of the United States in 1782.

Look For

Bald Eagles mate for life and renew pair bonds by adding sticks to their nests, which can be up to 15 ft in diameter, the largest of any North American bird.

Sharp-shinned Hawk
Accipiter striatus

After a successful hunt, the small Sharp-shinned Hawk often perches on a favorite "plucking post" with its meal in its razor-sharp talons. This hawk is a member of the *Accipiter* genus, or woodland hawks, and preys almost exclusively on small birds. Its short, rounded wings, long, rudderlike tail and flap-and-glide flight allow it to maneuver through the forest at high speed. • This hawk can be seen along the Blue Ridge Parkway and at Coastal refuges during migration.

Other ID: red eyes. *In flight:* short, rounded wings; dark barring on flight feathers.
Size: *Male: L* 10–12 in; *W* 20–24 in. *Female: L* 12–14 in; *W* 24–28 in.
Voice: usually silent; intense, repeated *kik-kik-kik-kik* during the breeding season.
Status: common migrant statewide; uncommon winter resident and breeder in the mountains and Piedmont.
Habitat: dense to semi-open forests and large woodlots; occasionally along rivers and in urban areas; favors dense, moist, coniferous forests for nesting.

Similar Birds

Cooper's Hawk

American Kestrel
(p. 62)

Merlin

blue-gray crown, back and upperwings

red horizontal bars on underparts

thin, white tail tip

immature

long, heavily barred, square-tipped tail

Nesting: in a conifer tree; builds a new stick nest or uses an abandoned crow nest; brown-blotched, bluish white eggs are 1½ x 1⅛ in; female incubates 4–5 eggs for 34–35 days; male feeds the female during incubation.

Did You Know?

As it ages, the Sharp-shinned Hawk's bright yellow eyes become red. This change may signal full maturity to potential mates.

Look For

During winter, Sharp-shinned Hawks may visit backyard bird feeders to prey on feeding sparrows and finches. Watch for their flap-and-glide flight pattern.

Red-tailed Hawk
Buteo jamaicensis

Take an afternoon drive through the country and look for Red-tailed Hawks soaring above the fields or perched along the road edges. Red-tails are the most common hawks in North Carolina, especially in winter. • In warm weather, these hawks use thermals and updrafts to soar. The pockets of rising air provide substantial lift, which allows migrating hawks to fly for almost 2 miles without flapping their wings. On cooler days, resident Red-tails perch on exposed tree limbs, fence posts or utility poles to scan for prey. Piedmont roadways in winter often host dozens of perched Red-tails scanning the right-of-way for prey.

Other ID: brown eyes; overall color varies geographically. *In flight:* fan-shaped tail; light underwing flight feathers with faint barring; dark leading edge on underside of wing.
Size: *Male: L* 18–23 in; *W* 4–5 ft. *Female: L* 20–25 in; *W* 4–5 ft.
Voice: powerful, raspy, descending scream: *keeearrr.*
Status: common statewide year-round.
Habitat: open country with some trees; also roadsides or woodlots.

Similar Birds

Broad-winged Hawk   Red-shouldered Hawk

dark shoulder
patches

juvenile

dark upperparts
with some white
highlights

dark brown band of
streaks across belly

red tail

Nesting: in woodlands adjacent to open habitat;
bulky stick nest is enlarged each year; brown-
blotched, whitish eggs are 2⅜ x 1⅞ in; pair incubates 2–4 eggs for 28–35 days.

Did You Know?

The Red-tailed Hawk's
piercing call is often
paired with the image of
an eagle in TV commer-
cials and movies.

Look For

Courting pairs will dive at
each other, lock talons and
tumble toward the earth.
Then they break away at the
last second to avoid crashing
into the ground.

American Kestrel
Falco sparverius

The colorful American Kestrel, formerly known as the "Sparrow Hawk," is one of the more easily seen birds of prey in North Carolina, especially in winter. Watch for this robin-sized bird along rural roadways, perched on poles and telephone wires or hovering over agricultural fields, foraging for insects and small mammals. • The kestrel was known as "Kitty Hawk" or "Killy Hawk" in earlier times, and the town of Kitty Hawk is named for this bird. • Look for kestrels along roadsides in the Coastal Plain in winter, and also at Mattamuskeet NWR, Alligator River NWR and Cape Hatteras National Seashore.

Other ID: *In flight:* long, rusty tail; frequently hovers; buoyant, indirect flight style.
Size: *L* 7½–8 in; *W* 20–24 in.
Voice: usually silent; loud, often repeated, shrill *killy-killy-killy* when excited; female's voice is lower pitched.
Status: common winter resident in coastal areas; fairly common migrant statewide; rare breeder (formerly common in the mountains and Piedmont regions).
Habitat: open fields, roadside ditches, grassy highway medians, grasslands and croplands.

Similar Birds

Merlin

Sharp-shinned Hawk
(p. 58)

blue-gray crown
with rusty cap

2 distinctive
facial stripes

dark barring
on rufous
back

rusty wings
and breast
streaking

blue-gray
wings

Nesting: in a tree cavity; may use a nest box; white to pale brown, spotted eggs are 1½ x 1⅛ in; mostly the female incubates 4–6 eggs for 29–30 days; both adults raise the young.

Did You Know?

The American Kestrel was the first falcon to reproduce by artificial insemination.

Look For

While hunting, the kestrel repeatedly lifts its tail while perched to scout below for prey.

Clapper Rail
Rallus longirostris

Although Clapper Rails are fairly common residents in some of North Carolina's coastal marshes, they have been extirpated from many other areas of the U.S. because of habitat loss. • The eggs of Clapper Rails hatch over the course of a few days. Young rails leave the nest within hours of hatching, so adults often split up—one parent stays on the nest to incubate any remaining eggs, while the other moves to a nearby area where the hatchlings are safely brooded. • This bird can be found at Cedar Island NWR, Fort Fisher SRA and Cape Hatteras National Seashore.

Other ID: long, slightly downcurved bill; 4 recognized subspecies differ in brightness of coloration.
Size: L 14½ in; W 19 in.
Voice: call is a series of 10 or more loud, harsh *kek* notes, accelerating at first, then slowing toward the end.
Status: common in salt marshes along the coast, becoming more common southward and in winter.
Habitat: tidal saltwater marshes of needle rush and cordgrass; often feed along marshy tidal channels during low tide.

Similar Birds

Virginia Rail

Least Bittern

King Rail

darker back feathers have
pale surrounding edges

grayish face

pale grayish brown
to cinnamon breast

gray to brown and
white barring on flanks

Nesting: in dense cover above or near water;
pair builds a cup nest of vegetation with a domed
canopy and an entrance ramp; pale buff, sparsely
spotted eggs are 1⅝ x 1¼ in; pair incubates 4–6
eggs for 20–24 days.

Did You Know?

One calling bird will often
cause an entire marsh to
erupt with the widely
scattered "chime-ins" of
other unseen rails.

Look For

The Clapper Rail character-
istically flicks its tail as it
walks, and it wades through
tidal marshes in search of
crayfish, crabs and other
prey.

American Coot
Fulica americana

Coots are weak fliers, and you might catch a glimpse of one rushing across the water, flailing its wings and splashing as it tries to lift off into flight.
• With feet that have individually webbed toes, the coot is adapted to diving, but it isn't afraid to steal a meal from another diver when a succulent piece of water celery is brought to the surface.
• Large flocks occur at coastal lakes, where they can form dense flocks of thousands of birds. Look for coots at Mattamuskeet NWR and Pocosin Lakes NWR.

Other ID: gray-black, ducklike bird; long, green-yellow legs; lobed toes; red eyes.
Size: L 13–16 in; W 24 in.
Voice: croaks and grunts in winter.
Status: abundant winter resident; fairly common on lakes across the state during migration; very rare breeder on large coastal lakes.
Habitat: shallow freshwater marshes, ponds and wetlands with open water and emergent vegetation; also sewage lagoons.

Similar Birds

Black Scoter   White-winged Scoter   Common Moorhen

reddish spot on white forehead "shield"

white marks on tail

white, chicken-like bill with dark ring around tip

Nesting: rare breeder in North Carolina; in emergent vegetation; pair builds floating nest of cattails and grass; buffy white, brown-spotted eggs are 2 x 1⅜ in; pair incubates 8–12 eggs for 21–25 days.

Did You Know?

The American Coot is the most widespread and abundant rail in North America.

Look For

Though this bird somewhat resembles a duck, a coot bobs its head while swimming or walking and has a narrower bill that extends up the forehead.

Black-bellied Plover
Pluvialis squatarola

These large plovers forage for small invertebrates with a robinlike run-and-stop technique, frequently pausing to lift their heads for a reassuring scan of their surroundings. They are usually found in coastal habitats but are equally comfortable foraging inland near fresh water. Watch for small flocks flashing their bold, white wing stripes as they fly low over the water's surface. • Black-bellied Plovers can be found at Cape Hatteras National Seashore and in agricultural areas of northeastern North Carolina, especially in winter.

Other ID: short, black bill; long, black legs. *Breeding:* black face, breast, belly and flanks; mottled, black and white back; white stripe leads from crown down "collar," neck and sides of breast.
Size: *L* 10½–13 in; *W* 29 in.
Voice: rich, plaintive, 3-syllable whistle: *pee-oo-ee,* usually given in flight.
Status: common on and near the coast, except early summer; rare inland during migration.
Habitat: coastal mudflats and beaches; plowed fields, sod farms and meadows; the edges of lakeshores and reservoirs.

Similar Birds

American
Golden-Plover

Look For

The Black-bellied Plover may forage with migrating American Golden-Plovers, which have black, instead of white, undertail coverts.

black "wing pits"

mottled, gray-brown upperparts

nonbreeding

bold, white wing linings

lightly streaked, pale underparts

nonbreeding

Nesting: does not nest in North Carolina; nests in the Arctic; on dry tundra; in a shallow depression lined with moss or lichen; cryptically colored eggs are 2 x 1½ in; pair incubates 4 eggs for about 27 days; both adults tend the young.

Did You Know?

The Black-belly is the largest North American plover. Whereas most plovers have three toes, the Black-belly has a fourth toe higher on its leg, similar to most sandpipers.

Killdeer
Charadrius vociferus

The Killdeer is a gifted actor, well known for its "broken wing" distraction display. When an intruder wanders too close to its nest, the Killdeer greets the interloper with piteous cries while dragging a wing and stumbling about as if injured. Most predators take the bait and follow, and once the Killdeer has lured the predator far away from its nest, it miraculously recovers from the injury and flies off with a loud call.
• Look for the Killdeer in short-grass areas around lighthouses on the Outer Banks in winter.

Other ID: brown head; white neck band; brown back and upperwings; white underparts; rufous rump. *Immature:* downy; only 1 breast band.
Size: *L* 9–11 in; *W* 24 in.
Voice: loud and distinctive *kill-dee kill-dee kill-deer;* variations include *deer-deer.*
Status: common year-round resident; less common in the mountains in winter.
Habitat: open areas, such as fields, lakeshores, sandy beaches, mudflats, gravel streambeds, wet meadows and grasslands.

Similar Birds

Semipalmated Plover

Piping Plover

Wilson's Plover

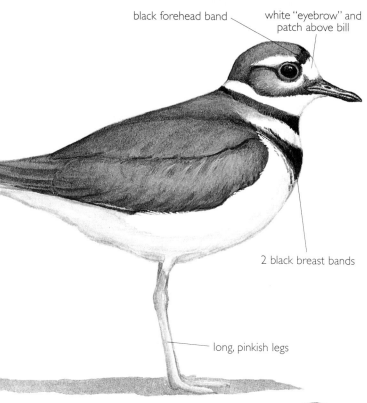

black forehead band

white "eyebrow" and patch above bill

2 black breast bands

long, pinkish legs

Nesting: on open ground; in a shallow, usually unlined depression; heavily marked, creamy buff eggs are 1⅜ x 1⅛ in; pair incubates 4 eggs for 24–28 days; may raise 2 broods.

Did You Know?

In spring, you might hear a European Starling imitate the vocal Killdeer's call.

Look For

The Killdeer has adapted well to urbanization, and it finds golf courses, gravel rooftops, farms, fields and abandoned industrial areas as much to its liking as shorelines.

American Oystercatcher

Haematopus palliatus

One of the few birds with a bill sturdy enough to pry open a mollusk shell, the American Oystercatcher eats a variety of shell-fish. When its taste buds cry out for more, it will gladly eat limpets, crabs, marine worms, sea urchins, chitons and even jellyfish. This large shorebird usually forages silently and alone, but it issues loud whistles as it flies between mud-flats and shellfish beds. • Oystercatchers can be found at Cape Hatteras National Seashore and the Wilmington area.

Other ID: *In flight:* bold white wing stripe and rump patch.
Size: *L* 18½ in; *W* 32 in.
Voice: call is a loud *wheet!*, often given in series during flight.
Status: fairly common permanent resident along the immediate coast; more common southward.
Habitat: coastal marine habitats, including saltwater marshes, sandy beaches and tidal mud-flats; will nest on dredge spoil islands.

Look For

During the summer breeding season, watch for amusing courtship displays. These birds issue loud "piping" calls while they run along together side by side, bobbing their heads up and down. They may also take to the air, still calling and maintaining proximity.

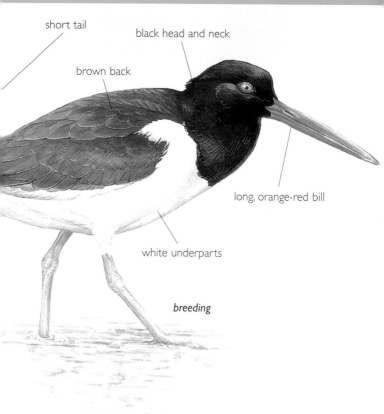

short tail

black head and neck

brown back

long, orange-red bill

white underparts

breeding

Nesting: scrape nest in sandy depression may be lined with dead plants, shells or pebbles; yellowish to brown, boldly marked eggs are 2¼ x 1½ in; pair incubates 2–4 eggs for 24–27 days; may mate for life.

Did You Know?

American Oystercatchers may form a breeding trio, with two females and one male. Together, the group tends up to two nests and takes care of the young for the first few weeks. The hatchlings are able to leave the nest and pick food a day or two after they are born.

Spotted Sandpiper

Actitis macularius

The female Spotted Sandpiper, unlike most other female birds, lays her eggs and leaves the male to tend the clutch. Free of responsibility, she flies off to mate again. Only about one percent of birds display this unusual breeding strategy known as polyandry. Each summer, the female can lay up to four clutches and is capable of producing 20 eggs.
• Look for this bird at Jordan Reservoir, Falls Lake and Lake Norman during spring and late summer into fall.

Other ID: teeters almost continuously. *Nonbreeding* and *immature:* pure white breast, foreneck and throat; brown bill; dull yellow legs.
Size: L 7–8 in; W 15 in.
Voice: sharp, crisp *eat-wheat, eat-wheat, wheat-wheat-wheat-wheat.*
Status: common migrant statewide; uncommon winter resident at coastal areas.
Habitat: shorelines, rivers, gravel beaches, drainage ditches, swamps and sewage lagoons; occasionally seen in cultivated fields.

Similar Birds

Solitary Sandpiper

Dunlin

white "eyebrow"

dark eye line

black-tipped, yellow orange bill

nonbreeding

short, white upperwing stripe

white underparts heavily spotted with black

yellow-orange legs

breeding

Nesting: breeding status in North Carolina poorly known; usually near water; sheltered by vegetation; shallow scrape is lined with grass; darkly blotched, creamy buff eggs are 1¼ x 1 in; male incubates 4 eggs for 20–24 days.

Did You Know?

Sandpipers have four toes: three point forward and one points backward. Most plovers, such as the Killdeer, have only three toes.

Look For

Spotted Sandpipers bob their tails constantly on shore and fly with rapid, shallow, stiff-winged strokes.

Sanderling
Calidris alba

This lucky shorebird graces sandy shorelines around the world. The Sanderling runs and chases the waves, snatching up aquatic invertebrates before they are swept back into the water. It will also probe mudflats for a meal of mollusks and insects. • At times the Sanderling will take a rest from its zigzag dance along a beach to stand with one leg tucked up, a posture that conserves body heat. • Cape Hatteras National Seashore and Fort Fisher are good locations for spotting Sanderlings.

Other ID: *Breeding:* dark mottling on rufous head, breast and upperparts; white underparts. *Nonbreeding:* black shoulder patch (often concealed). *In flight:* dark leading edge of wing.
Size: L 7–8½ in; W 17 in.
Voice: flight call is a sharp *kip* or *plick*.
Status: common on sandy shores along the entire coast year-round and on mudflats at inlets.
Habitat: sandy and muddy shorelines, cobble and pebble beaches, spits, lakeshores, marshes and reservoirs.

Similar Birds

Baird's Sandpiper

Least Sandpiper

White-rumped Sandpiper

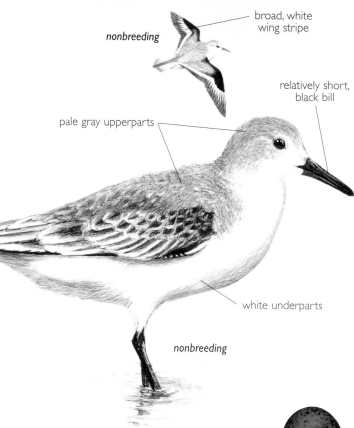

nonbreeding

broad, white
wing stripe

relatively short,
black bill

pale gray upperparts

white underparts

nonbreeding

Nesting: does not nest in North Carolina; nests in the Arctic; on the ground; cup nest is lined with leaves; brown-blotched, olive eggs are 1½ x 1 in; pair incubates 3–4 eggs for 23–24 days.

Did You Know?

The Sanderling is widespread, breeding across the Arctic and wintering on whatever continent it chooses, excluding Antarctica.

Look For

Sanderlings in pale nonbreeding plumage reflect a ghostly glow as they forage at night on moonlit beaches.

Laughing Gull
Larus atricilla

Laughing Gulls were nearly extirpated from the Atlantic Coast in the late 19th century, when egg collecting was popular and feathers for women's hats were in high demand. East Coast populations have gradually recovered, and Laughing Gulls are once again common along North Carolina's coastline. They are frequently seen loitering in parking lots, around beaches or following ferries, as they keep a sharp eye out for leftovers.

Other ID: *Nonbreeding:* white head with some pale gray bands; black bill. *Immature:* variable plumage; brown to gray and white overall; broad, black subterminal tail band.
Size: *L* 15–17 in; *W* 3 ft.
Voice: loud, high-pitched, laughlike call: *ha-ha-ha-ha-ha-ha.*
Status: common in summer; fairly common in winter on the coast and uncommon at inland sites during migration.
Habitat: primarily coastal in bays and estuaries; salt marshes and sandy beaches; occasionally inland shores, streams, agricultural lands or landfills.

Similar Birds

Bonaparte's Gull

Common Tern

black head

broken, white
eye ring

nonbreeding

red bill

breeding

Nesting: colonial nester; on a dry island, sandy coastal beach or in a salt marsh; pair builds a cup nest of marsh vegetation on ground; darkly blotched, olive buff eggs are 2¼ x 1½ in; pair incubates 3 eggs for 22–27 days.

Did You Know?

Nesting colonies on small offshore islands are vulnerable to spring storms and high tides that flood shoreline nests.

Look For

The Latin name *atricilla*, "black tail," refers to a black band present only on the tails of immature birds.

Herring Gull
Larus argentatus

First discovered nesting in North Carolina in 1962, these large gulls have become common along the coast, often associating with other gulls. These handsome birds are often seen soaring along the edge of coastal bridges over large rivers and sounds, using the deflected wind currents to fly effortlessly in search of a meal. • Herring Gulls can be found at Cape Hatteras National Seashore and Cape Lookout, and at Fort Fisher SRA in winter.

Other ID: yellow bill; light eyes; light gray mantle; white underparts. *Nonbreeding:* white head and nape are washed with brown. *In flight:* white-spotted, black wing tips.
Size: *L* 23–26 in; *W* 4 ft.
Voice: loud, buglelike *kleew-kleew;* also an alarmed *kak-kak-kak.*
Status: common along the coast year-round; more common on the northern half of the coast during the breeding season; uncommon inland migrant.
Habitat: large lakes, wetlands, rivers, landfills and urban areas.

Similar Birds

Ring-billed Gull

Glaucous Gull

nonbreeding

white head

red spot on
lower mandible

pink legs

breeding

Nesting: singly or colonially; on an open beach or island; in a shallow scrape lined with vegetation and sticks; darkly blotched, olive to buff eggs are 2¾ x 1⅞ in; pair incubates 3 eggs for 31–32 days.

Did You Know?

Nestlings use the small red spot on the gull's lower bill as a target. A hungry chick will peck at the spot, cueing the parent to regurgitate its meal.

Look For

The Herring Gull has pink legs and a red bill spot, whereas the similar-looking Ring-billed Gull has yellow legs and a black band around its bill.

Royal Tern
Sterna maxima

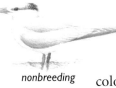

nonbreeding

Female Royal Terns lay a single egg (or occasionally two) amid a tightly packed colony of up to 10,000 nests. Both adults take responsibility for incubating their treasure through hot, sun-drenched days, cool coastal nights and brutal summer storms. Most of the eggs in the colony hatch within a few days of each other, turning the beach colony into a raucous muddle of commotion. • Look for this tern at Cape Hatteras National Seashore, Cape Lookout and in the Wilmington area.

Other ID: *Nonbreeding:* frayed black fringe at back of head. *In flight:* deeply forked tail; thick, dark wedge on tips of upperwings.
Size: *L* 20 in; *W* 3½ ft.
Voice: bleating call is a high-pitched *kee-er;* also gives a whistling *turreee.*
Status: common permanent resident along the coast.
Habitat: coastal habitats, including sandy beaches, estuaries, saltwater marshes, islands, bays and lagoons.

Similar Birds

Caspian Tern

Look For

During the breeding season, the male Royal Tern performs spiraling aerial flights, then struts in front of the female with offerings of fish.

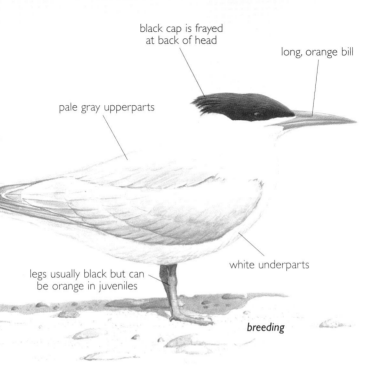

black cap is frayed
at back of head

long, orange bill

pale gray upperparts

white underparts

legs usually black but can
be orange in juveniles

breeding

Nesting: colony nester; usually on sandy
ground; shallow depression is unlined or lined
sparsely with vegetation; heavily marked, ivory
eggs are 2½ x 1¾ in; pair incubates 1–2 eggs
for 20–25 days.

Did You Know?

Parenting terns shepherd their young into a massive herd
of fluffy, hungry newborns known as a "creche." Supervised
by incoming squadrons of food-carrying adults, the creche
remains well protected while adults hunt continuously
for food.

Black Skimmer
Rynchops niger

nonbreeding

The Black Skimmer is the only bird in North America with a lower mandible that is longer than its upper mandible. The skimmer plows its scoop-like lower mandible just below the water's surface feeling for fish, then slams its upper mandible down, clamping the slippery prey securely within its bill.

• Unmistakable Black Skimmers propel themselves through the air on long, swept-back wings, flying low over shallow water.

Other ID: *Nonbreeding:* white collar and duller upperparts. *Immature:* dull, mottled brown upperparts.
Size: *L* 18 in; *W* 3¾ ft.
Voice: call is a series of yapping notes.
Status: fairly common summer resident along the coast; fairly common winter species in southern half of the coast; species of special concern.
Habitat: coastal marine habitats, including estuaries, lagoons, sheltered bays and inlets.

Look For

Black Skimmers may feed at any time of the day or night, but they usually forage most actively at low tide and 2 hours before high tide.

long, thick, red bill with black tip (lower mandible longer than upper mandible)

black upperparts

white underparts

breeding

Nesting: colony nester; on beaches, sandy islands and rarely on gravel roofs; nest is a shallow scraped depression in sand; boldly blotched, white eggs are 1¾ x 1½ in; mainly female incubates 3–4 eggs for 21–23 days.

Did You Know?

At hatching, the mandibles of a baby Black Skimmer's bill are equal in length. As the bird matures, the lower mandible grows at a faster rate than the upper mandible.

Rock Pigeon
Columba livia

The colorful and familiar Rock Pigeons have an unusual feature: they feed their young a substance similar to milk. These birds lack mammary glands, but they produce a nutritious liquid, called "pigeon milk," in their crops. A chick inserts its bill down the adult's throat to reach the thick, protein-rich fluid. • This pigeon is likely a descendant of a Eurasian bird that was first domesticated about 4500 BC. The Rock Pigeon was introduced to North America in the 17th century by settlers.

Other ID: *In flight:* holds wings in a deep "V" while gliding.
Size: *L* 12–13 in; *W* 28 in (male is usually larger).
Voice: soft, cooing *coorrr-coorrr-coorrr*.
Status: common in urban areas and along interstates at overpasses; less common in the mountains.
Habitat: urban areas, railroad yards and agricultural areas.

Similar Birds

Mourning Dove
(p. 88)

Eurasian
Collared-Dove

color is highly variable
(iridescent, blue-gray,
red, white or tan)

usually has white rump

white cere

orange feet

Nesting: in a barn or on a cliff, bridge or tower; in a flimsy nest of sticks, grass and other vegetation; glossy white eggs are 1½ x 1⅛ in; pair incubates 2 eggs for 16–19 days; may raise broods year-round.

Did You Know?

Much of our understanding of bird migration, color genetics and sensory perception comes from experiments involving Rock Pigeons.

Look For

No other "wild" bird varies as much in coloration, a result of semidomestication and extensive inbreeding over time.

Mourning Dove
Zenaida macroura

The Mourning Dove's soft cooing, which filters through broken woodlands and suburban parks, is often confused with the sound of a hooting owl. Curious birders who track down the source of the calls are often surprised to find the streamlined silhouette of a perched dove. • This popular game animal is one of the most abundant native birds in North America. Its numbers and range have increased since human development created more open habitats and food sources, such as bird feeders. Mourning Doves are especially plentiful in agricultural areas in fall as young and adults flock together to feed on waste grain.

Other ID: buffy, gray-brown plumage; small head; dark bill; sleek body; dull red legs.
Size: *L* 11–13 in; *W* 18 in.
Voice: mournful, soft, slow *oh-woe-woe-woe*.
Status: common permanent resident across North Carolina.
Habitat: open and riparian woodlands, forest edges, open parks and agricultural and suburban areas.

Similar Birds

Rock Pigeon
(p. 86)

Yellow-billed Cuckoo
(p. 91)

Eurasian
Collared-Dove

pale blue eye ring

dark, shiny patches below ear

pale rosy underparts

long, white-trimmed, tapering tail

black spots on upperwing

Nesting: in a shrub or tree; occasionally on the ground; nest is a fragile, shallow platform of twigs; white eggs are 1⅛ x ⅞ in; pair incubates 2 eggs for 14 days.

Did You Know?

The Mourning Dove raises up to six broods each year—more than any other native bird.

Look For

When the Mourning Dove bursts into flight, its wings clap above and below its body. It also often creates a whistling sound as it flies at high speed.

Yellow-billed Cuckoo
Coccyzus americanus

Large tracts of hardwood forest such as those in the Coastal Plain, river bottomland swamps of the Piedmont and river systems of the mountains provide important habitat for the Yellow-billed Cuckoo. • Songbirds are increasingly vulnerable to predators in the fragmented forests left behind by human development. The sycamore and riparian habitat of the cuckoo has also deteriorated over the years as waterways are altered or dammed. • Good sites for viewing this bird include the New River drainage area, Cape Fear basin, Alligator River NWR and the French Broad River basin.

Other ID: olive brown upperparts; white underparts.
Size: L 11–13 in; W 18 in.
Voice: long series of deep, hollow *kuks*, slowing near the end: *kuk-kuk-kuk-kuk kuk kop kow kowlp kowlp*.
Status: fairly common breeder but not normally found above 3500 ft in the mountains, where it is replaced by the Black-billed Cuckoo; common migrant at all elevations.
Habitat: semi-open deciduous habitats; dense tangles and thickets at the edges of orchards, urban parks and river corridors; sometimes in woodlots.

Similar Birds

Black-billed Cuckoo

Mourning Dove
(p. 88)

yellow eye ring

long tail with large
white spots on
underside

mainly yellow,
downcurved bill with
black upper ridge

rufous tinge on
primaries

Nesting: on a low horizontal branch in a
deciduous shrub or small tree, flimsy platform
nest of twigs is lined with grass; pale bluish green
eggs are 1 1/4 x 7/8 in; pair incubates 3–4 eggs for
9–11 days.

Did You Know?

Yellow-billed Cuckoos lay
larger clutches when out-
breaks of cicadas or tent
caterpillars provide an
abundant food supply.

Look For

The Yellow-billed Cuckoo, or
"Rain Crow," has a propen-
sity for calling on dark,
cloudy days and a reputation
for predicting rain storms.

Eastern Screech-Owl

Megascops asio

red morph

The diminutive Eastern Screech-Owl is a year-round resident of mid- and low-elevation deciduous woodlands. • Most screech-owls sleep away the daylight hours snuggled safely inside tree cavities or artificial nest boxes. The noise of a mobbing horde of chickadees or a squawking gang of Blue Jays can alert you to an owl's presence during the day. • Unique among North Carolina owls, the Eastern Screech-Owl shows both red and gray color morphs. The gray morph is more common in the eastern part of the state, and the red morph seems to be more common in the mountains. Very rarely, an intermediate brown morph occurs.

Other ID: reddish or grayish overall; yellow eyes; pale grayish bill.
Size: *L* 8–9 in; *W* 20–22 in.
Voice: horselike "whinny" that rises and falls.
Status: common and widespread permanent resident across the state.
Habitat: mature deciduous forests, open deciduous and riparian woodlands, orchards and shade trees with natural cavities; also woodlots near open areas, city parks and state parks.

Similar Birds

Northern
Saw-whet Owl

Long-eared Owl

short "ear" tufts

dark breast streaking

gray morph

Nesting: in a natural cavity or artificial nest box; no lining is added; white eggs are 1½ x 1⅜ in; female incubates 4–5 eggs for about 26 days; male brings food to the female during incubation.

Did You Know?

Adaptable screech-owls have one of the most varied diets of any owl, capturing small animals, earthworms and insects.

Look For

Eastern Screech-Owls respond readily to whistled imitations of their calls, and sometimes several owls will appear to investigate the fraudulent perpetrator.

Great Horned Owl
Bubo virginianus

This highly adaptable and superbly camouflaged hunter has sharp hearing and powerful vision that allow it to hunt at night as well as by day. It will swoop down from a perch onto almost any small creature that moves. • Owls have specially designed feathers on their wings to reduce noise. The leading edge of the flight feathers is fringed rather than smooth, which interrupts airflow over the wings and allows owls to fly noiselessly. • Great Horned Owls begin their courtship as early as December (when calling is most common), and by January and February the females are already incubating their eggs.

Other ID: overall plumage varies from light gray to dark brown; heavily mottled, gray, brown and black upperparts; yellow eyes; white "chin."
Size: L 18–25 in; W 3–5 ft.
Voice: breeding call is 4–6 deep hoots: *hoo-hoo-hoooo hoo-hoo* or *Who's awake? Me too;* female gives lower-pitched hoots.
Status: common permanent resident statewide.
Habitat: fragmented forests, fields, riparian woodlands, suburban parks and wooded edges of landfills.

Similar Birds

Long-eared Owl

Eastern Screech-Owl
(p. 92)

tall, widely spaced "ear" tufts form a triangle with beak

rusty orange facial disc is outlined in black

fine, horizontal barring on breast

Nesting: in another bird's abandoned stick nest or in a tree cavity; adds little or no nest material; dull whitish eggs are 2¼ x 1⅞ in; mostly the female incubates 2–3 eggs for 28–35 days.

Did You Know?

The Great Horned Owl has a poor sense of smell, which might explain why it is the only consistent predator of skunks.

Look For

Owls regurgitate pellets that contain the indigestible parts of their prey. You can find these pellets, which are generally clean and dry, under frequently used perches.

Barred Owl
Strix varia

The adaptable Barred Owl is found in many wood-land habitats throughout our state, especially those near water. It prefers large tracts of mature forest, ranging from swampy bottomlands to higher, mixedwood forests in the Great Smoky Mountains. • Each spring, the escalating laughs, hoots and gar-gling howls of Barred Owls reinforce pair bonds. These owls tend to be more vocal during late evening and early morning when the moon is full, the air is calm and the sky is clear. • Look for this owl at Lake Mattamuskeet NWR, Jordan Lake SRA and Falls Lake SRA.

Other ID: mottled, dark gray-brown plumage.
Size: L 17–24 in; W 3½–4 ft.
Voice: loud, hooting, rhythmic, laughlike call is heard mostly in spring: *Who cooks for you? Who cooks for you all?*
Status: common permanent resident in bottomland swamps and cove forests; uncommon in other habitats.
Habitat: mature coniferous and mixedwood forests, especially in dense stands near swamps, streams and lakes.

Similar Birds

Great Horned Owl
(p. 94)

Short-eared Owl

no "ear" tufts

dark eyes

pale bill

horizontal barring around neck and upper breast

vertical streaking on belly

Nesting: in a natural tree cavity, broken treetop or abandoned stick nest; adds very little material to the nest; white eggs are 2 x 1⅝ in; female incubates 2–3 eggs for 28–33 days.

Did You Know?

In darkness, the Barred Owl's eyesight may be 100 times that of humans, and it is also able to locate and follow prey using sound alone.

Look For

Dark eyes make the Barred Owl unique—most familiar large owls in North America have yellow eyes.

Chuck-will's-widow
Caprimulgus carolinensis

The Chuck-will's-widow patrols the evening skies for insects while endlessly whistling its own name. Tiny, stiff "rictal bristles" encircle this bird's bill and funnel prey into its large mouth as it flies. This bird's yawning gape allows it to capture flying insects of all sizes. Occasionally, the Chuck-will's-widow will even take a small bird! • This perfectly camouflaged bird is virtually undetectable during the day, roosting on a horizontal tree limb or sitting among scattered leaves on the forest floor. It can be found at Goose Creek SP, Fort Fisher SRA and Croatan NF.

Other ID: long, rounded tail. *Male:* inner edges of outer tail feathers are white. *Gray morph:* plain gray crown; dark spots on overall gray body. *In flight:* long, pointed wings.
Size: *L* 12 in; *W* 26 in.
Voice: 3 loud, whistling notes, often paraphrased as *chuck-will's-widow*.
Status: common summer resident in coastal sections; uncommon in the Piedmont; absent from the mountains.
Habitat: riparian woodlands, swamp edges and deciduous and pine woodlands.

Similar Birds

Whip-poor-will

Common Nighthawk

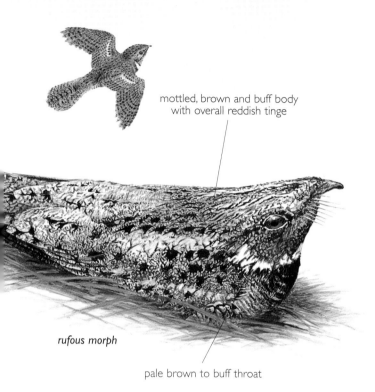

mottled, brown and buff body
with overall reddish tinge

rufous morph

pale brown to buff throat

Nesting: on bare ground; no nest is built; heavily
blotched, creamy white eggs are 1⅜ x 1 in;
female incubates 2 eggs for about 21 days and
raises young alone.

Did You Know?

Members of the nightjar
family can eat thousands
of insects a day.

Look For

Nightjars' eyes mirror light,
so watching for reflected
points of orange or red light
may help you find these
birds while they are roosting
on the ground.

Chimney Swift
Chaetura pelagica

Chimney Swifts are the "frequent fliers" of the bird world—they feed, drink, bathe, collect nest material and even mate while they fly! They spend much of their time catching insects in the skies above our urban neighborhoods. • In fall in North Carolina, large flocks of migrating swifts assemble at large chimneys to roost. Chimney Swifts have small, weak legs and cannot take flight again if they land on the ground. For this reason, swifts usually cling to vertical surfaces with their strong claws. • Elementary school chimneys are favorite migrant roosts in September.

Other ID: brown overall; slim body. *In flight:* rapid wingbeats; boomerang-shaped profile; erratic flight pattern.
Size: *L* 5–5½ in; *W* 12–13 in.
Voice: call is a rapid *chitter-chitter-chitter* given in flight; also gives a rapid series of staccato *chip* notes.
Status: abundant breeder and migrant.
Habitat: forages above cities and towns, especially during breeding season; roosts and nests in chimneys; may nest in tree cavities in more remote areas.

Similar Birds

Northern Rough-winged Swallow

Bank Swallow

Cliff Swallow

long, thin, pointed, crescent-shaped wings

squared tail

Nesting: often colonial; half-saucer nest of short twigs is attached to a vertical wall; white eggs are ¾ x ½ in; pair incubates 4–5 eggs for 19–21 days.

Did You Know?

Migrating Chimney Swifts have a long migration, flying all the way to Peru!

Look For

Swifts frequently nest in brick chimneys or abandoned buildings and use saliva to attach their half-saucer nests to the walls.

Ruby-throated Hummingbird

Archilochus colubris

Ruby-throated Hummingbirds bridge the ecological gap between birds and bees—they feed on sweet, energy-rich flower nectar and pollinate flowers in the process. A sugarwater feeder or native nectar-producing flowers such as honeysuckle can attract hummingbirds to your backyard. • Each year, Ruby-throated Hummingbirds migrate across the Gulf of Mexico—a nonstop, 500-mile journey—in spring and again in fall. They may lose up to a third of their body mass while making this flight.

Other ID: thin, needlelike bill; pale underparts.
Size: *L* 3½–4 in; *W* 4–4½ in.
Voice: a loud *chick* and other high squeaks; soft buzzing of the wings while in flight.
Status: fairly common breeder; abundant late summer and early fall migrant, especially near the coast.
Habitat: open, mixed woodlands, wetlands, orchards, tree-lined meadows, flower gardens and backyards with trees and feeders, especially near patches of favored native foods (bee balm, jewelweed, trumpet vine, etc.).

Look For

Hummingbirds are among the few birds that can fly vertically and in reverse. When hummingbirds hover, their unique, flexible wings move forward and backward, rather than up and down, as if tracing a figure 8.

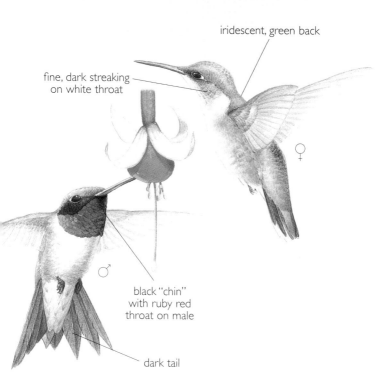

iridescent, green back

fine, dark streaking
on white throat

♀

black "chin"
with ruby red
throat on male

♂

dark tail

Nesting: on a horizontal tree limb; tiny, deep cup nest of plant down and fibers is held together with spider silk; lichens and leaves are pasted on the exterior walls; white eggs are $\frac{1}{2} \times \frac{3}{8}$ in; female incubates 2 eggs for 13–16 days.

Did You Know?

Weighing about as much as a nickel, a hummingbird can briefly reach speeds of up to 60 mph. In straight-ahead flight, hummingbirds beat their wings up to 80 times per second, and their hearts can beat up to 1200 times per minute!

Belted Kingfisher
Ceryle alcyon

Perched on a bare branch over a productive pool, the Belted Kingfisher utters a scratchy, rattling call. Then, with little regard for its scruffy hairdo, the "king of the fishers" plunges headfirst into the water to snag a fish or frog. Back on its perch, the kingfisher flips its prey into the air and swallows it headfirst. Similar to owls, kingfishers regurgitate the indigestible portion of their food as pellets, which can be found beneath favorite perches.
• Nestlings have closed eyes and are featherless for the first week, but after five days they are able to swallow small fish whole. • Look for kingfishers perched on power lines over ditches along roads.

Other ID: bluish upperparts; small white patch near eye; straight bill; short legs; white underwings.
Size: *L* 11–14 in; *W* 20–21 in.
Voice: fast, repetitive, cackling rattle, like a teacup shaking on a saucer.
Status: common permanent resident; less common in the mountains in winter.
Habitat: rivers, large streams, lakes, marshes and beaver ponds, especially near exposed soil banks, gravel pits or bluffs; coastal areas in winter.

Similar Birds

Blue Jay (p. 122)

Look For

The female Belted Kingfisher, with her rust-colored band across her chest, exhibits "reverse sexual dimorphism," which means she is more colorful than the male, a rare avian characteristic.

shaggy crest

white "collar"

♀

♂

rust-colored "belt"
on female may be
incomplete

blue-gray
breast band

Nesting: in a cavity at the end of an earth burrow; glossy white eggs are 1⅜ x 1 in; pair incubates
6–7 eggs for 22–24 days.

Did You Know?

Kingfisher pairs nest on sandy banks, taking turns digging a
tunnel with their sturdy bills and claws. Nest burrows may
measure up to 6 ft long and are often found near water.
Once the young are at least five days old, the parents return
to the nest regularly with small fingerling fish.

Red-bellied Woodpecker
Melanerpes carolinus

The familiar Red-bellied Woodpecker is no stranger to suburban backyards and will sometimes nest in birdhouses. • These birds often issue noisy, rolling *churr* calls as they poke around wooded landscapes in search of seeds, fruit and a variety of insects. Unlike most woodpeckers, Red-bellies consume large amounts of plant material, seldom excavating wood for insects. • This woodpecker can be found at Jordan Lake SRA and Falls Lake SRA.

Other ID: reddish tinge on bell; white patches on topside base of primaries. *Juvenile:* dark gray crown; streaked breast.
Size: L 9–10½ in; W 16 in.
Voice: call is a soft, rolling *churr;* drums in second-long bursts.
Status: fairly common permanent resident statewide but only at lower elevations in the mountains.
Habitat: mature deciduous woodlands, especially bottomland hardwoods; occasionally in wooded residential areas.

Similar Birds

Northern Flicker
(p. 110)

Red-headed Woodpecker

black and white barring on back

red nape extends to forehead

red nape

♂

white patches on rump

♀

Nesting: in woodlands or residential areas; in a cavity excavated mainly by the male; white eggs are 1 x ¾ in; pair incubates 4–5 eggs for 12–14 days.

Did You Know?

Studies of banded Red-bellied Woodpeckers have shown that these birds have a lifespan in the wild of more than 20 years.

Look For

The more common Red-bellied Woodpecker is often mistaken for a Red-headed Woodpecker, which has an entirely red head.

Downy Woodpecker

Picoides pubescens

A bird feeder well stocked with peanut butter
and peanut hearts may attract a pair of Downy
Woodpeckers to your backyard. These approach-
able little birds are more tolerant of human activity
than most other species, and they visit feeders
more often than the larger, more aggressive Hairy
Woodpeckers (*P. villosus*). • Like other woodpeckers, the Downy has evolved special features to help
cushion the shock of repeated hammering, including a strong bill and neck muscles, a flexible, rein-
forced skull and a brain that is tightly packed in its
protective cranium.

Other ID: black eye line and crown; white belly.
Male: small, red patch on back of head. *Female:* no
red patch.
Size: L 6–7 in; W 12 in.
Voice: long, unbroken trill; calls are a sharp *pik* or
ki-ki-ki or whiny *queek queek*.
Status: common permanent resident.
Habitat: any wooded environment,
especially deciduous and mixed
forests, areas with tall, deciduous
shrubs and woodlots.

Similar Birds

Hairy Woodpecker

Yellow-bellied
Sapsucker

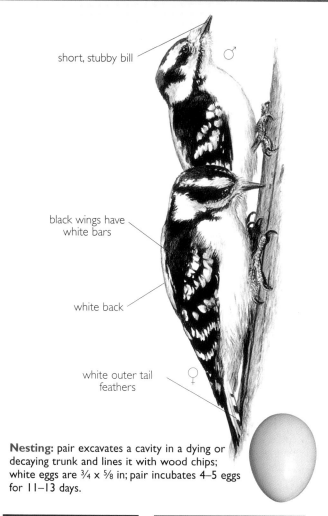

short, stubby bill

♂

black wings have white bars

white back

white outer tail feathers

♀

Nesting: pair excavates a cavity in a dying or decaying trunk and lines it with wood chips; white eggs are ¾ x ⅝ in; pair incubates 4–5 eggs for 11–13 days.

Did You Know?

Woodpeckers have feathered nostrils that filter out the sawdust produced by hammering.

Look For

The Downy Woodpecker uses its small bill to probe tiny crevices for invertebrates and wood-boring grubs.

Northern Flicker
Colaptes auratus

Northern Flickers are widespread in the mountains, especially along the Blue Ridge Parkway during the breeding season, and can be found in coastal parks and refuges during winter. • Flickers often bathe in dusty depressions. The dust particles absorb oils and bacteria that can harm the birds' feathers. To clean themselves even more thoroughly, flickers, and most other birds, squash captured ants and preen themselves with the remains. Ants contain formic acid, which kills small parasites on the flickers' skin and feathers.

Other ID: long bill; brownish to buff face; gray crown; white rump. *Male:* black "mustache" stripe. *Female:* no "mustache."
Size: *L* 12–13 in; *W* 20 in.
Voice: loud, rapid, laughlike *kick-kick-kick-kick-kick-kick; woika-woika-woika* issued during courtship.
Status: common permanent resident.
Habitat: *Breeding:* open woodlands and forest edges, fields, meadows, beaver ponds and other wetlands. *In migration* and *winter:* coastal vegetation, offshore islands, urban gardens.

Similar Birds

Red-bellied
Woodpecker (p. 106)

Yellow-bellied
Sapsucker

brown, black-barred
back and wings

♂

black-spotted,
buff to whitish
underparts

red nape crescent

black "bib"

♀

yellow underwings
and undertail

"Yellow-shafted"

Nesting: pair excavates a cavity in a dying or decaying trunk and lines it with wood chips; may also use a nest box; white eggs are 1⅛ x ⅞ in; pair incubates 5–8 eggs for 11–16 days.

Did You Know?

The very long tongue of a woodpecker wraps around twin structures in the skull and is stored like a measuring tape in its case.

Look For

Instead of boring holes in trees, Northern Flickers scour the ground in search of invertebrates, particularly ants.

Pileated Woodpecker
Dryocopus pileatus

The Pileated Woodpecker, with its flaming red crest, chisel-like bill and commanding size, requires 100 acres or more of mature forest as a home territory. In North Carolina, the patchwork of woodlots and small towns limits the availability of continuous habitat, requiring this woodpecker to show itself more. • A pair will spend up to six weeks excavating a large nest cavity in a dead or decaying tree. Other birds and even flying squirrels frequently nest in abandoned Pileated Woodpecker cavities. • Good sites for spotting this bird are Lake Mattamuskeet, the Blue Ridge Parkway and Great Smoky Mountains NP.

Other ID: predominantly black; yellow eyes; white "chin." *Male:* red "mustache." *Female:* no red "mustache"; gray-brown forehead.
Size: L 16–17 in; W 28–29 in.
Voice: loud, fast, rolling *woika-woika-woika-woika;* long series of *kuk* notes; loud, resonant drumming.
Status: fairly common to common year-round in wooded areas; less common in the Piedmont.
Habitat: extensive tracts of mature forests; also riparian woodlands or woodlots in suburban and agricultural areas.

Similar Birds

Yellow-bellied
Sapsucker

Red-headed
Woodpecker

Red-bellied
Woodpecker (p. 106)

flaming red crest extends farther on male

stout, dark bill

♂

white stripe runs from bill to shoulder

♀

white wing linings

Nesting: pair excavates a cavity in a dying or decaying trunk and lines it with wood chips; white eggs are 1¼ x 1 in; pair incubates 4 eggs for 15–18 days.

Did You Know?

A woodpecker's bill becomes shorter as the bird ages, so juvenile birds have slightly longer bills than adults.

Look For

Foraging Pileated Woodpeckers leave large, rectangular cavities up to 12 in long at the base of trees.

Acadian Flycatcher
Empidonax virescens

The Acadian Flycatcher's speedy, aerial courtship chases and the male's hovering flight displays are sights to behold—that is if you can survive the swarming hordes of bloodsucking mosquitoes deep within the swampy woodlands where this flycatcher is primarily found. • Floodplain forests in the Piedmont and Coastal Plain and hemlock coves in the mountains provide preferred nest sites for the Acadian Flycatcher. Look for this flycatcher at New River SP, Jordan Reservoir, the Roanoke River basin and the Cape Fear basin.

Other ID: large bill has dark upper mandible and pinkish yellow lower mandible; faint olive yellow breast; yellow belly and undertail coverts.
Size: L 5½–6 in; W 9 in.
Voice: song is a forceful *peet-sa;* call is a softer *peet;* may issue a loud, flickerlike *ti-ti-ti-ti-ti* during the breeding season.
Status: fairly common summer resident except above 4000 ft in elevation; widespread in floodplain forests.
Habitat: fairly mature deciduous woodlands, riparian woodlands and wooded swamps.

Similar Birds

Alder Flycatcher

Willow Flycatcher

Least Flycatcher

Eastern
Wood-Pewee

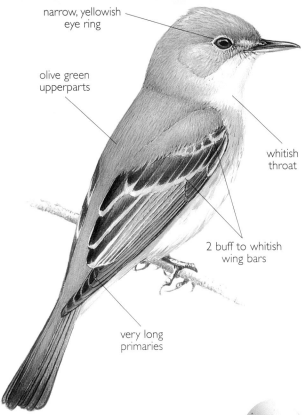

narrow, yellowish eye ring

olive green upperparts

whitish throat

2 buff to whitish wing bars

very long primaries

Nesting: low in a deciduous tree, or a conifer in the mountains; female builds a loose cup nest of plants and spider silk; white, lightly spotted eggs are $^{11}/_{16}$ x $^{9}/_{16}$ in; female incubates 2–4 eggs for 13–15 days.

Did You Know?

Flycatchers are members of the family *Tyrannidae*, or "Tyrant Flycatchers," so named because of their feisty, aggressive behavior.

Look For

A standing dead tree or "planted" tree limb in your backyard may attract flycatchers that are looking for a hunting perch.

Great Crested Flycatcher

Myiarchus crinitus

Loud, raucous calls give away the presence of the brightly colored Great Crested Flycatcher. This large flycatcher often inhabits forest edges and nests in woodlands throughout North Carolina. It can be found at Alligator River NWR and Jordan Reservoir. • Unlike other eastern flycatchers, the Great Crested prefers to nest in a tree cavity or an abandoned woodpecker hole, or even a nest box. Once in a while, it will decorate the nest entrance with a shed snakeskin or substitute translucent plastic wrap. The purpose of this practice is not fully understood, though it might make any would-be predators think twice.

Other ID: dark olive brown upperparts; heavy black bill.
Size: L 8–9 in; W 13 in.
Voice: loud, whistled *wheep!* and a rolling *prrrrreet!*
Status: fairly common summer resident in the mountains; common summer resident in the Piedmont and Coastal Plain; rare winter visitor near the coast.
Habitat: deciduous and mixed woodlands and forests, usually near openings or edges.

Similar Birds

Eastern Phoebe

Eastern Kingbird
(p. 118)

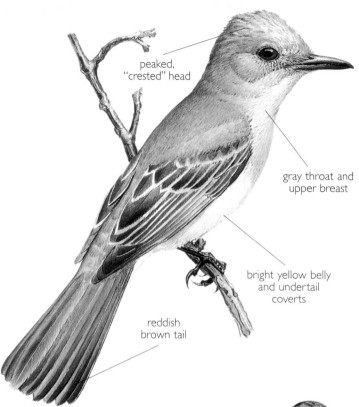

peaked, "crested" head

gray throat and upper breast

bright yellow belly and undertail coverts

reddish brown tail

Nesting: in a tree cavity or artificial cavity lined with grass; may hang a shed snakeskin over entrance hole; lightly spotted, pale eggs are 7/8 x 5/8 in; female incubates 5 eggs for 13–15 days.

Did You Know?

Many animals depend on tree cavities for shelter and nesting, so instead of cutting down large, dead trees, consider leaving a few standing.

Look For

Follow the loud *wheep!* calls and watch for a show of bright yellow and rufous feathers to find this fly-catcher.

Eastern Kingbird
Tyrannus tyrannus

This bird is sometimes referred to as the "Jekyll and Hyde" bird, because it is a gregarious fruit eater while wintering in South America and an antisocial, aggressive insect eater while nesting in North America. The Eastern Kingbird fearlessly attacks crows, hawks and even humans that pass through its territory, pursuing and pecking at them until the threat has passed. No one familiar with the Eastern Kingbird's pugnacious behavior will refute its scientific name, *Tyrannus tyrannus*. This bird reveals a gentler side of its character in a quivering, butterfly-like courtship flight.

Other ID: black bill and legs; no eye ring; white underparts; grayish breast.
Size: *L* 8½–9 in; *W* 15 in.
Voice: call is a quick, loud, chattering *kit-kit-kitter-kitter;* also a *buzzy dzee-dzee-dzee.*
Status: in summer, common in the Piedmont and fairly common in the mountains and Coastal Plain along rivers and in open agricultural areas; common migrant in fall on the coast.
Habitat: fields with scattered shrubs, trees or hedgerows, forest fringes, clearings, shrubby road-sides, towns and farmyards.

Similar Birds

Olive-sided Flycatcher

Eastern Wood-Pewee

Eastern Phoebe

small head crest

thin orange-red crown
(rarely seen)

dark gray to black
upperparts

white-tipped tail

Nesting: on a horizontal limb, stump or upturned tree root; cup nest is made of weeds, twigs and grass; darkly blotched, white to pinkish white eggs are 1 x ¾ in; female incubates 3–4 eggs for 14–18 days.

Did You Know?

Eastern Kingbirds rarely walk or hop on the ground—they prefer to fly, even for very short distances.

Look For

These flycatchers are common and widespread. On a drive in the country you will likely spot at least one of these birds sitting on a fence or utility wire.

Red-eyed Vireo

Vireo olivaceus

Capable of delivering about 40 phrases per minute, the male Red-eyed Vireo can outsing any one of his courting neighbors. One tenacious male set a record by singing 21,000 phrases in one day! Although you may still hear the Red-eyed Vireo singing five or six hours after other songbirds have ceased for the day, this bird is not easy to spot. It is usually concealed in its olive brown plumage among the foliage of deciduous trees. Its unique red eyes, unusual among songbirds, are even trickier to spot without a good pair of binoculars.

Other ID: black-bordered, olive "cheek"; olive green upperparts; white to pale gray underparts.
Size: *L* 6 in; *W* 10 in.
Voice: call is a short, scolding *rreeah. Male:* song is a series of quick, continuous, variable phrases with pauses in between: *look-up, way-up, tree-top, see-me, here-I-am!*
Status: common summer resident statewide; widespread in forested tracts, abundant in the mountains, especially along the Blue Ridge Parkway and in Great Smoky Mountains NP.
Habitat: deciduous or mixed woodlands with a shrubby understory.

Similar Birds

Philadelphia Vireo

Warbling Vireo

Tennessee Warbler

blue-gray crown

white "eyebrow"

red eyes

dark eye line

breeding

Nesting: in a tree or shrub; hanging cup nest is made of grass, roots, spider silk and cocoons; darkly spotted, white eggs are ¾ x ½ in; female incubates 4 eggs for 11–14 days.

Did You Know?

If its nest is parasitized by a Brown-headed Cowbird, a Red-eyed Vireo will respond by abandoning its nest or raising the cow-bird young with its own.

Look For

The Red-eyed Vireo perches with a hunched stance and hops with its body turned diagonally to its direction of travel.

Blue Jay

Cyanocitta cristata

The Blue Jay is the only member of the corvid family that is dressed in blue in North Carolina. It is easily recognizable with its white-flecked wing feathers and sharply defined facial features. It can be quite aggressive when competing for sunflower seeds and peanuts at backyard feeding stations and rarely hesitates to drive away smaller birds, squirrels or even cats when it feels threatened. Even the Great Horned Owl is not too formidable a predator for a group of these brave, boisterous mobsters to harass.

Other ID: blue upperparts; white underparts; black bill.
Size: *L* 11–12 in; *W* 16 in.
Voice: noisy, screaming *jay-jay-jay;* nasal *queedle queedle queedle-queedle* sounds like a muted trumpet; often imitates various sounds, including calls of other birds.
Status: common permanent resident.
Habitat: mixed deciduous forests, agricultural areas, scrubby fields and townsites.

Similar Birds

Belted Kingfisher
(p. 104)

Eastern Bluebird
(p. 138)

blue crest

white bars and flecking on wings

black "necklace"

dark bars and white corners on blue tail

Nesting: in a tree or tall shrub; pair builds a bulky stick nest; greenish, buff or pale eggs, spotted with gray and brown are 1⅛ x ¾ in; pair incubates 4–5 eggs for 16–18 days.

Did You Know?

Blue Jays store food from feeders in trees and other places for later use.

Look For

Large migrating flocks of 50 or more Blue Jays may be seen in spring and fall.

American Crow
Corvus brachyrhynchos

The noise that most often emanates from this tree-top squawker seems unrepresentative of its intelligence. However, this wary, clever bird is also an impressive mimic, able to whine like a dog and laugh or cry like a human. • American Crows have flourished in spite of considerable efforts, over many generations, to reduce their numbers. One of the reasons for this species' staying power is that it is a generalist, which allows it to adapt to a variety of habitats, food types and changing environmental conditions.

Other ID: black bill and legs; square-shaped tail.
Size: L 17–21 in; W 3 ft.
Voice: distinctive, far-carrying, repetitive *caw-caw-caw*.
Status: abundant permanent resident statewide.
Habitat: urban areas, agricultural fields and other open areas with scattered woodlands.

Similar Birds

Common Raven

Common Grackle

slim, sleek head
and throat

glossy, purple-black plumage

Nesting: in a tree or on a utility pole; large stick-and-branch nest is lined with fur and soft plant material; darkly blotched, gray-green to blue-green eggs are 1⅝ x 1⅛ in; female incubates 4–6 eggs for about 18 days.

Did You Know?

Crows are family oriented, and the young from the previous year may help their parents to raise the nestlings.

Look For

To distinguish this bird from the Common Raven, look for the squared tail and slimmer bill of the American Crow and listen for the deeper croak of the raven.

Purple Martin
Progne subis

These large swallows will entertain you throughout spring and summer if you set up luxurious "condo complexes" for them. Martin adults spiral around their accommodations in pursuit of flying insects, while the young perch clumsily at the cavity openings. Purple Martins once nested in natural tree hollows and in cliff crevices, but they now have virtually abandoned these in favor of human-made housing. • These birds can be seen at Coastal Plain and Piedmont sites near rural houses where birdhouses or gourds have been erected; roost sites in late summer include the old Highway 64 bridge in Dare County.

Other ID: pointed wings; small bill. *Female:* sooty gray underparts.
Size: *L* 7–8 in; *W* 18 in.
Voice: rich, fluty, robinlike *pew-pew*, often heard in flight.
Status: common summer resident in the Piedmont and coastal areas; abundant migrant in late summer near traditional roost sites; scarce in the mountains.
Habitat: semi-open areas, often near water.

Similar Birds

European Starling
(p. 150)

Barn Swallow
(p. 128)

Tree Swallow

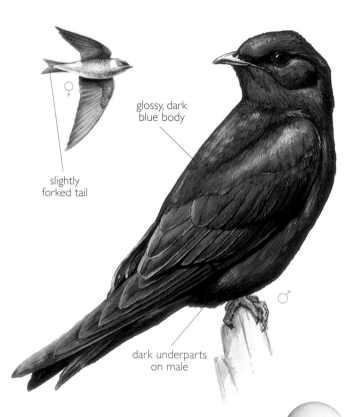

glossy, dark
blue body

slightly
forked tail

♀

♂

dark underparts
on male

Nesting: communal; in a birdhouse or hollowed-out gourd; nest is made of feathers, grass and mud; white eggs are 1 x ⅝ in; female incubates 4–5 eggs for 15–18 days.

Did You Know?

The Purple Martin is North America's largest swallow and congregates in late summer at communal roosts of several thousand birds.

Look For

You will have better success attracting Purple Martins to your martin condo complex if it is erected in an open area, high on a pole and near a body of water.

Barn Swallow
Hirundo rustica

When you encounter this bird, you might first notice its distinctive, deeply forked tail—or you might just find yourself repeatedly ducking to avoid the dives of a protective parent. Barn Swallows once nested on cliffs, but they are now found more frequently nesting on barns, boat-houses and areas under bridges and house eaves. The messy young and aggressive parents unfortunately often bring people to remove nests just as nesting season is beginning, but this bird's close association with humans allows us to observe the normally secretive reproductive cycle of birds.

Other ID: blue-black upperparts; long, pointed wings.
Size: *L* 7 in; *W* 15 in.
Voice: continuous, twittering chatter: *zip-zip-zip* or *kvick-kvick*.
Status: common throughout North Carolina.
Habitat: open rural and urban areas where bridges, culverts and buildings are found near water.

Similar Birds

Cliff Swallow

Purple Martin
(p. 126)

Tree Swallow

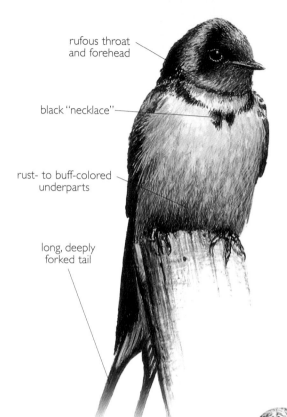

rufous throat
and forehead

black "necklace"

rust- to buff-colored
underparts

long, deeply
forked tail

Nesting: singly or in small, loose colonies; on a
human-made structure under an overhang; half
or full cup nest is made of mud, grass and straw;
brown-spotted, white eggs are ¾ x ½ in; pair
incubates 4–7 eggs for 13–17 days.

Did You Know?

The Barn Swallow is a
natural pest controller,
feeding on insects that
are often harmful to
crops and livestock.

Look For

Barn Swallows roll mud into
small balls and build their
nests one mouthful of mud
at a time.

Carolina Chickadee
Poecile carolinensis

Fidgety, friendly Carolina Chickadees are familiar to anyone with a backyard feeder well stocked with sunflower seeds and peanut butter. Like some woodpeckers and nuthatches, the Carolina Chickadee will hoard food for later seasons when food may become scarce. • Come breeding season, this energetic little bird can be found hammering out a hollow in a rotting tree. Occasionally a chickadee will also nest in an abandoned woodpecker hole or birdhouse. • Where the ranges of the Carolina Chickadee and Black-capped Chickadee *(P. atricapillus)* overlap in the Appalachians, the Carolina Chickadee tends to stick to lower elevations.

Other ID: white underparts; buffy flanks.
Size: L 4¾ in; W 7½ in.
Voice: whistling song has 4 clear notes: *fee-bee fee-bay.*
Status: common permanent resident statewide, except scarce or absent on the Outer Banks.
Habitat: deciduous and mixed woods, riparian woodlands, groves and isolated shade trees; frequents urban areas.

Similar Birds

Black-capped Chickadee

White-breasted Nuthatch (p. 130)

Blackpoll Warbler

black cap and bib

white "cheek"

gray upperparts and secondaries

Nesting: excavates or enlarges a tree cavity; may also use a nest box; cavity is lined with soft material; white eggs, marked with reddish brown are $9/16$ x $7/16$ in; female incubates 5–8 eggs for 11–14 days.

Did You Know?

Alert Carolina Chickadees are often the first to issue alarm calls, warning other birds that danger is near.

Look For

Each fall, adult Carolina Chickadees tour the neighborhood, introducing their offspring to the best feeding spots.

Tufted Titmouse
Baeolophus bicolor

This bird's amusing feeding antics and its insatiable appetite keep curious observers entertained at bird feeders. Grasping an acorn or sunflower seed with its tiny feet, the dexterous Tufted Titmouse will strike its dainty bill repeatedly against the hard outer coating to expose the inner core. • The Tufted Titmouse nests in tree cavities that have been excavated and then abandoned by woodpeckers. A snakeskin hanging over the entrance of a nest may catch your eye—some titmice engage in this unusual habit, possibly to deter predators.

Other ID: white underparts; pale face.
Size: L 6–6½ in; W 10 in.
Voice: noisy, scolding call, like that of a chickadee; song is a whistled *peter peter* or *peter peter peter*.
Status: common permanent resident statewide, except scarce or absent on the Outer Banks.
Habitat: deciduous woodlands, groves and suburban parks with large, mature trees.

Look For

A breeding pair will maintain their bond throughout the year, even when joining small, mixed flocks in winter. The family bond is so strong that the young from one breeding season will often stay with their parents long enough to help them with nesting and feeding duties the following year.

gray crest and upperparts

black forehead

gray upperparts

buffy flanks

Nesting: in a natural cavity or woodpecker cavity lined with soft vegetation, moss and animal hair; heavily spotted, white eggs are $^{11}/_{16}$ x $^{9}/_{16}$ in; female incubates 5–6 eggs for 12–14 days.

Did You Know?

Nesting pairs search for soft nest-lining material in late winter and may accept an offering of the hair that has accumulated in your hairbrush.

White-breasted Nuthatch

Sitta carolinensis

A combination of upside-down antics and a noisy, nasal *yank-hank yank-hank* call make the White-breasted Nuthatch a favorite among novice birders. • Comparing the White-breasted Nuthatch to the Carolina Chickadee, both regular visitors to feeders, is a perfect starting point for introductory birding. While these similar-sized cavity nesters both have dark crowns and gray backs, the nuthatch's foraging behaviors and undulating flight pattern are distinctive.

Other ID: white underparts and face; straight bill; short legs. *Male:* black "cap." *Female:* dark gray "cap."
Size: L 5½–6 in; W 11 in.
Voice: song is a fast, nasal *yank-hank yank-hank*, lower than the Red-breasted Nuthatch; calls include *ha-ha-ha ha-ha-ha*, *ank ank* and *ip*.
Status: common permanent resident.
Habitat: mixedwood forests, woodlots and backyards.

Similar Birds

Red-breasted Nuthatch

Carolina Chickadee
(p. 130)

Brown-headed Nuthatch

rusty undertail coverts

gray-blue back

short tail

dark crown

♀

♂

Nesting: in a natural cavity or an abandoned wood-pecker nest; female lines the cavity with soft material; white eggs, speckled with brown are ¾ x ⁹/₁₆ in; female incubates 5–8 eggs for 12–14 days.

Did You Know?

Nuthatches are presumably named for their habit of wedging seeds and nuts into crevices and hacking them open with their bills.

Look For

Nuthatches grasp trees through foot power alone, unlike woodpeckers, which use their tails to brace themselves against tree trunks.

Carolina Wren
Thryothorus ludovicianus

The energetic and cheerful Carolina Wren can be shy and retiring, often hiding deep inside dense shrubbery. The best opportunity for viewing this large wren is when it sits on a conspicuous perch while unleashing its impressive song. Pairs perform lively "duets" at any time of day and in any season. The duet often begins with introductory chatter by the female, followed by innumerable ringing variations of *tea-kettle tea-kettle tea-kettle tea* from her mate. • Carolina Wrens readily nest in the brushy thickets of an overgrown backyard or in an obscure nook or crevice in a house or barn. If conditions are favorable, two broods may be raised in a single season.

Other ID: white throat; slightly downcurved bill.
Size: *L* 5½ in; *W* 7½ in.
Voice: loud, repetitious *tea-kettle tea-kettle tea-kettle tea* may be heard at any time of day or year; female often chatters while male sings.
Status: common permanent resident statewide.
Habitat: dense forest undergrowth, especially shrubby tangles and thickets; also near houses and developed areas.

Similar Birds

House Wren

Winter Wren

Red-breasted Nuthatch

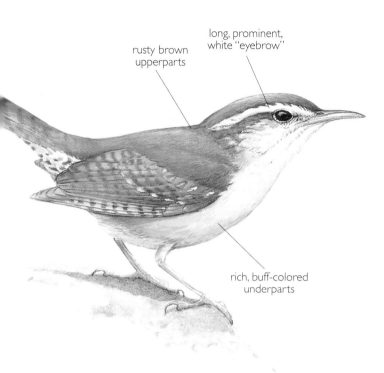

rusty brown
upperparts

long, prominent,
white "eyebrow"

rich, buff-colored
underparts

Nesting: in a nest box or natural or artificial cavity; nest is lined with soft material, including snakeskin at the entrance; brown-blotched, white eggs are ¾ x ⁹⁄₁₆ in; female incubates 4–5 eggs for 12–16 days.

Did You Know?

In mild winters, Carolina Wren populations remain stable, but frigid temperatures can temporarily decimate an otherwise healthy population.

Look For

Carolina Wrens often use human-made structures and items for nest sites, including hanging baskets on porches and cans or buckets in open sheds and garages.

Eastern Bluebird
Sialia sialis

This cavity nester's survival has been put to the test in the past—populations have declined in the presence of the competitive, introduced House Sparrow and European Starling. The removal of standing dead trees has also diminished nest site availability. Thankfully, bluebird enthusiasts and organizations have developed "bluebird trails" and mounted nest boxes on fence posts along highways and rural roads, allowing Eastern Bluebird numbers to gradually recover. Good spots to look for this beautiful bird include the Blue Ridge Parkway, Falls Lake and Howell Woods.

Other ID: dark bill and legs. *Female:* thin, white eye ring; gray-brown head and back tinged with blue; blue wings and tail; paler chestnut underparts.
Size: L 7 in; W 13 in.
Voice: song is a rich, warbling *turr, turr-lee, turr-lee;* call is a chittering *pew.*
Status: common permanent resident.
Habitat: cropland fencelines, meadows, fallow and abandoned fields, pastures, forest clearings and edges, golf courses, large lawns and cemeteries.

Similar Birds

Blue Grosbeak

Indigo Bunting
(p. 172)

deep blue
upperparts

chestnut red
"chin," throat
and sides

♂

white belly and
undertail coverts

Nesting: in a natural cavity or nest box; female builds a cup nest of grass, weed stems and small twigs; pale blue eggs are ⅞ x ⅝ in; female incubates 4–5 eggs for 13–16 days.

Did You Know?

This bird's blue color is the result of the microstructure of the feathers, which causes scattering of some wavelengths of light.

Look For

Bluebirds have straight, pointed bills that are perfect for capturing insects. They also feed on berries and are especially attracted to wild grapes, sumac and currants.

Wood Thrush
Hylocichla mustelina

The loud, warbled notes of the Wood Thrush once resounded through our woodlands, but forest fragmentation and urban sprawl have eliminated much of this bird's nesting habitat. Broken forests and diminutive woodlots have allowed for the invasion of common, open-area predators and parasites, such as raccoons, skunks, crows, jays and cowbirds. Traditionally, these predators had little access to nests that were hidden deep within vast hardwood forests. This bird can be found in Great Smoky Mountains NP and along the Blue Ridge Parkway.

Other ID: plump body; streaked "cheeks"; brown wings, rump and tail.
Size: *L* 8 in; *W* 13 in.
Voice: *Male:* bell-like phrases of 3–5 notes, with each note at a different pitch and followed by a trill: *Will you live with me? Way up high in a tree, I'll come right down and...seeee!;* calls include a *pit pit* and *bweebeebeep.*
Status: common summer resident statewide up to 4000 ft in elevation.
Habitat: moist, mature and preferably undisturbed deciduous woodlands and mixed forests.

Similar Birds

Brown Thrasher
(p. 148)

Swainson's Thrush

Veery

bold, white eye ring

rusty head and back

large black spots on white breast, sides and flanks

Nesting: low in a fork of a deciduous tree; female builds a bulky cup nest of vegetation, held together with mud and lined with softer material; pale greenish blue eggs are 1 x ¾ in; female incubates 3–4 eggs for 13–14 days.

Did You Know?

Henry David Thoreau considered the Wood Thrush's song to be the most beautiful of avian sounds. The male can even sing two notes at once!

Look For

Wood Thrushes forage on the ground or glean vegetation for insects and other invertebrates.

American Robin
Turdus migratorius

Come March, the familiar song of the American Robin may wake you early if you are a light sleeper. This abundant bird adapts easily to urban areas and often works from dawn until after dusk when there is a nest to be built or hungry, young mouths to feed. • The robin's bright red belly contrasts with its dark head and wings and makes the robin easy to identify. Robins gather in huge flocks along our coast in winter, and they used to be harvested for food by some coastal communities.

Other ID: incomplete, white eye ring; gray-brown back; white undertail coverts.
Size: *L* 10 in; *W* 17 in.
Voice: song is an evenly spaced warble: *cheerily cheer-up cheerio;* call is a rapid *tut-tut-tut.*
Status: common permanent resident; more abundant along the coast in winter; less common near the coast in summer.
Habitat: *Breeding:* residential lawns and gardens, pastures, urban parks, broken forests, bogs and river shorelines. *Winter:* near fruit-bearing trees and wetlands.

Similar Birds

Orchard Oriole
(p. 180)

Look For

A hunting robin with its head tilted to the side isn't listening for prey—it is actually looking for movements in the soil.

black head

white throat is streaked with black

dark gray head

black-tipped, yellow bill

♂   ♀

brick red breast is darker on male

Nesting: in a tree or shrub; cup nest is built of grass, moss, bark and mud; light blue eggs are 1⅛ x ¾ in; female incubates 4 eggs for 11–16 days; raises up to 3 broods per year.

Did You Know?

American Robins do not use nest boxes; they prefer platforms for their nests. Robins usually raise two broods per year, and the male cares for the fledglings from the first brood while the female incubates the second clutch of eggs.

Gray Catbird

Dumetella carolinensis

This accomplished mimic may fool you if you hear it shuffling through underbrush and dense riparian shrubs, calling its catlike *meow*. Its mimicking talents are further enhanced by its ability to sing two notes at once, using each side of its syrinx individually. • In a competitive nesting habitat of sparrows, robins and cowbirds, the Gray Catbird will vigilantly defend its territory. It will destroy the eggs and nestlings of other songbirds and will take on an intense defensive posture if approached, screaming and even attempting to hit an intruder.

Other ID: dark gray overall; black eyes, bill and legs.
Size: *L* 8½–9 in; *W* 11 in.
Voice: calls include a catlike *meow* and a harsh *check-check;* song is a variety of warbles, squeaks and mimicked phrases interspersed with a *mew* call.
Status: common permanent resident statewide but as a breeder and migrant in the mountains and Piedmont, and breeder, migrant and winter resident in the Coastal Plain.
Habitat: dense thickets, brambles, shrubby or brushy areas and hedgerows, often near water.

Similar Birds

Northern Mockingbird
(p. 146)

Look For

If you catch a glimpse of this bird during breeding season, watch the male raise his long slender tail into the air to show off his rust-colored undertail coverts.

black cap

long, dark gray
to black tail

rust-colored
undertail coverts

Nesting: in a dense shrub or thicket; bulky cup nest is made of twigs, leaves and grass; greenish blue eggs are 7/8 x 5/8 in; female incubates 4 eggs for 12–15 days.

Did You Know?

Female catbirds are very loyal to their nests, so Gray Catbirds are less prone to parasitism by Brown-headed Cowbirds. Even if a cowbird sneaks past the watchful female to deposit an egg in the nest, she recognizes the foreign egg and immediately ejects it.

Northern Mockingbird

Mimus polyglottos

Northern Mockingbirds are great entertainers with a lot to say. Their amazing vocal repertoire includes over 400 different song types, which they belt out incessantly during breeding season. Mockingbirds can imitate almost anything, from the vocalizations of other birds and animals to musical instruments.
• Look for the Northern Mockingbird in semi-open areas around houses and developments, especially in the Piedmont.

Other ID: gray upperparts; 2 thin, white wing bars; light gray underparts. *In flight:* large white patch at base of black primaries.
Size: *L* 10 in; *W* 14 in.
Voice: song is a medley of mimicked phrases, often repeated 3 times or more; calls include a harsh *chair* and *chewk*.
Status: common permanent resident, becoming more common as a breeder in the mountains.
Habitat: hedges, suburban gardens and orchard margins with an abundance of available fruit; hedgerows of roses are especially important in winter.

Similar Birds

Loggerhead Shrike

Gray Catbird
(p. 144)

long, dark tail with white outer tail feathers

thin, dark eye line

dark wings

Nesting: often in a small shrub or tree; cup nest is built with twigs and plants; brown-blotched, bluish gray to greenish eggs are 1 x ⅝ in; female incubates 3–4 eggs for 12–13 days.

Did You Know?

The scientific name *poly-glottos* is Greek for "many tongues" and refers to this bird's ability to mimic a wide variety of sounds.

Look For

Offerings of suet, raisins and fruit at feeders can lure these and other birds into your yard.

Brown Thrasher
Toxostoma rufum

The Brown Thrasher shares the streaked breast of a thrush and the long tail of a catbird, but it has a temper of its own. Because it nests close to the ground, the Brown Thrasher defends its nest with a vengeance, attacking snakes and other nest robbers, sometimes to the point of drawing blood. • Biologists have estimated that the male Brown Thrasher is capable of producing up to 3000 distinctive song phrases—the most extensive vocal repertoire of any North American bird.

Other ID: reddish brown upperparts and long, rufous tail; orange-yellow eyes.
Size: L 11½ in; W 13 in.
Voice: sings a large variety of phrases, with each phrase usually repeated twice: *dig-it dig-it, hoe-it hoe-it, pull-it-up pull-it-up.*
Status: common permanent resident; becoming more abundant at the coast in winter; uncommon in winter in the mountains; more abundant as a breeder in the Piedmont.
Habitat: dense shrubs and thickets, overgrown pastures, woodland edges and brushy areas, rarely close to urban areas.

Similar Birds

Hermit Thrush

Wood Thrush
(p. 140)

long, downcurved bill

gray "cheek"

2 white wing bars

pale underparts with heavy, brown streaking

Nesting: usually in a low shrub; often on the ground; cup nest of grass, twigs and leaves is lined with vegetation; pale blue eggs, dotted with reddish brown are 1 x ¾ in; pair incubates 4 eggs for 11–14 days.

Did You Know?

Shrubby, wooded areas bordering wetlands and streams can be fenced to prevent cattle from devastating thrasher nesting habitat.

Look For

The Brown Thrasher can be hard to find in its shrubby understory habitat. You might catch only a flash of rufous as it flies from one thicket to another.

European Starling

Sturnus vulgaris

The European Starling did not hesitate to make itself known across North America after being released in New York's Central Park in 1890 and 1891. This highly adaptable bird not only took over the nest sites of native cavity nesters, such as Tree Swallows and Red-headed Woodpeckers, but it also learned to mimic the sounds of Killdeers, Red-tailed Hawks, Soras and meadowlarks. • Look for European Starlings in massive evening roosts under bridges or on buildings in winter.

Other ID: dark eyes; short, squared tail. *Nonbreeding:* feather tips are heavily spotted with white and buff.
Size: *L* 8½ in; *W* 16 in.
Voice: variety of whistles, squeaks and gurgles; imitates other birds.
Status: common permanent resident statewide.
Habitat: cities, towns, residential areas, farmyards, woodland fringes and clearings, especially developed areas with short grass, such as yards, highway medians and golf courses.

Similar Birds

Brown-headed Cowbird (p. 178)

Red-winged Blackbird (p. 174)

iridescent, purple-black
head, neck and breast

glossy, green back
with buffy spots

yellow bill

greenish black
underparts

breeding

Nesting: in an abandoned woodpecker cavity, natural cavity or nest box; nest is made of grass, twigs and straw; bluish to greenish white eggs are 1⅛ x ⅞ in; female incubates 4–6 eggs for 12–14 days.

Did You Know?

This bird was brought to New York as part of the local Shakespeare society's plan to introduce all the birds mentioned in their favorite author's writings.

Look For

Sometimes confused with a blackbird, the European Starling has a shorter tail and a bright yellow bill.

Yellow-rumped Warbler

Dendroica coronata

This species comes in two forms: the common, white-throated "Myrtle Warbler" of the East, and the yellow-throated "Audubon's Warbler" of the West, which is very rare in North Carolina. Although Myrtles do not breed in North Carolina, they are commonly seen in winter.
• This bird can be found in coastal areas with bayberry and wax myrtle, including Cape Hatteras National Seashore and the Wilmington area.

Other ID: thin, white eye line, strong streaking on underparts; white corners on tail.
Size: L 5½ in; W 9¼ in.
Voice: male's song is a brief, bubbling warble, rising or falling at the end; much variation; call is a sharp *chip* or *chet*.
Status: abundant winter resident and migrant at the coast; common migrant and winter resident elsewhere; but less common in the mountains in winter.
Habitat: a variety of well-vegetated habitats in lowlands, especially in wax myrtle thickets.

Similar Birds

Black-throated Green Warbler

Palm Warbler

Pine Warbler

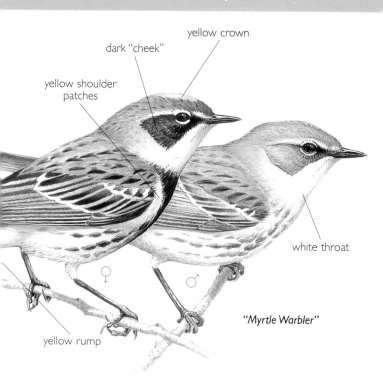

yellow crown

dark "cheek"

yellow shoulder patches

white throat

yellow rump

♀

♂

"Myrtle Warbler"

Nesting: not known to nest in North Carolina; nests in the western and northern U.S. and in Canada; in a crotch or on a horizontal limb in a conifer; cup nest is made of vegetation and spider silk; brown-blotched, buff-colored eggs are ⅝ x ½ in; female incubates 4–5 eggs for up to 13 days.

Did You Know?

This small warbler's habit of flitting near buildings to snatch spiders from their webs has earned it the nickname "Spider Bird."

Look For

Small puddles that form during or after rains often attract warblers, which like to bathe in the fresh water, allowing us a glimpse of these secretive birds.

Ovenbird
Seiurus aurocapilla

Even the sharpest human eye will have trouble spotting the Ovenbird's immaculately concealed nest along hiking trails and bike paths. An incubating female is usually confident enough in the camouflage of her ground nest that she will choose to sit tight rather than flee in the presence of danger. Despite these evolutionary adaptations, forest fragmentation and Brown-headed Cowbird parasitism have reduced this bird's nesting success. • Look for the Ovenbird along the Blue Ridge Parkway and in Great Smoky Mountains NP.

Other ID: olive brown upperparts; no wing bars; white undertail coverts; pink legs.
Size: *L* 6 in; *W* 9½ in.
Voice: loud, distinctive *tea-cher tea-cher Tea-CHER Tea-CHER,* increasing in speed and volume; night song is a set of bubbly, warbled notes, often ending in *teacher-teacher;* call is a brisk *chip, cheep* or *chock.*
Status: widespread and common migrant; common summer resident in the mountains; becoming less common east to the upper Coastal Plain.
Habitat: *Breeding:* undisturbed, mature forests with a closed canopy and little understory. *In migration:* dense riparian shrubs and thickets.

Similar Birds

Louisiana Waterthrush   Northern Waterthrush   Wood Thrush
(p. 140)

rufous crown
bordered by black

white eye ring

heavy, dark streaking
on white breast, sides
and flanks

Nesting: on the ground; female builds a domed, oven-shaped nest of grass, twigs, bark and dead leaves, lined with animal hair; gray and brown-spotted, white eggs are $\frac{3}{4}$ x $\frac{1}{2}$ in; female incubates 4–5 eggs for 11–13 days.

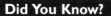

Did You Know?

The name Ovenbird refers to this bird's unusual ground nest which is shaped like a brick oven.

Look For

In summer, this bird remains hidden in tangles of low shrubs or among conifer branches. However, the male's loud *tea-cher* song gives away his presence.

Common Yellowthroat

Geothlypis trichas

The bumblebee colors of the male's black "mask" and yellow throat identify this skulking wetland resident. The cattail outposts from which he perches to sing his *witchety* song are strategically chosen, and he visits them in rotation, fiercely guarding his territory against the intrusion of other males. • The Common Yellowthroat prefers marshlands and wet, overgrown meadow. Good sites for this bird are Falls Lake, Jordan Reservoir, Lake Mattamuskeet and the Wilmington area.

Other ID: black bill; orange legs. *Female:* may show faint, white eye ring.
Size: L 5 in; W 7 in.
Voice: song is a clear, oscillating *witchety witchety witchety-witch;* call is a sharp *tcheck* or *tchet.*
Status: common summer resident in the mountains; fairly common winter resident in the Coastal Plain; uncommon in winter in the Piedmont.
Habitat: coastal areas, wetlands, riparian areas and wet, overgrown meadows; sometimes dry fields.

Similar Birds

Wilson's Warbler

Nashville Warbler

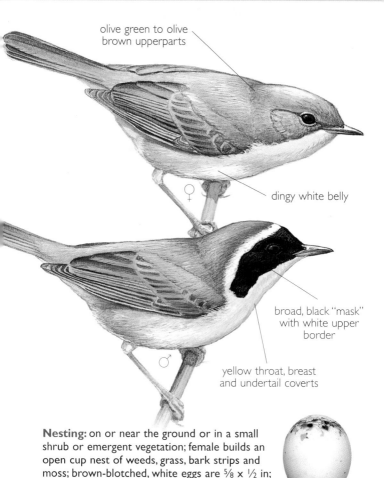

olive green to olive brown upperparts

dingy white belly

broad, black "mask" with white upper border

yellow throat, breast and undertail coverts

Nesting: on or near the ground or in a small shrub or emergent vegetation; female builds an open cup nest of weeds, grass, bark strips and moss; brown-blotched, white eggs are ⅝ x ½ in; female incubates 3–5 eggs for 12 days.

Did You Know?

Famous Swedish biologist Carolus Linnaeus named the Common Yellowthroat in 1766, making it one of the first North American birds to be documented.

Look For

Common Yellowthroats immerse themselves or roll in water to bathe, then shake off the excess water by flicking or flapping their wings.

Scarlet Tanager
Piranga olivacea

The vibrant red of a breeding male Scarlet Tanager may catch your eye in North Carolina's forests and migrant stopover sites. Because this tanager is more likely to reside in forest canopies, birders tend to hear the Scarlet Tanager before they see it. Its song, a sort of slurred version of the American Robin's, is a much-anticipated sound that announces the arrival of this colorful long-distance migrant. • The Scarlet Tanager family moves from the forest interior where it breeds to more shrubby habitats after the young have fledged. • Look for these birds along the Blue Ridge Parkway and in Great Smoky Mountains NP.

Other ID: *Female:* uniformly olive upperparts; yellow underparts; grayish brown wings; yellow eye ring.
Size: L 7 in; W 11½ in.
Voice: song is a series of 4–5 sweet, clear, whistled phrases; call is *chip-burrr* or *chip-churrr.*
Status: common summer resident in the mountains; fairly common summer resident in the Piedmont; rare migrant in the Coastal Plain.
Habitat: fairly mature, upland deciduous and mixed forests; also coastal shrubbery in migration.

Similar Birds

Summer Tanager

Northern Cardinal
(p. 168)

pale bill

pure black wings and tail

bright red body

♀

♂

breeding

Nesting: high in a deciduous tree; female builds a flimsy, shallow cup nest of grass, weeds and twigs; brown-spotted, pale blue green-eggs are ⅞ x ⅝ in; female incubates 2–5 eggs for 12–14 days.

Did You Know?

In Central and South America, there are over 200 tanager species in every color imaginable.

Look For

Male Scarlet Tanagers often find an exposed sunny perch from which to sing early in the breeding season, which makes them easier to see.

Eastern Towhee
Pipilo erythrophthalmus

Eastern Towhees are large, colorful members of the sparrow family. These noisy birds are often heard before they are seen as they rustle about in dense undergrowth, craftily scraping back layers of dry leaves to expose the seeds, berries or insects hidden beneath. They employ an unusual two-footed technique to uncover food items—a strategy that is especially important in winter when virtually all of their food is taken from the ground.
• Towhees can be found along the Blue Ridge Parkway and at Falls Lake and Jordan Reservoir.

Other ID: white outer tail corners, lower breast and belly; buff undertail coverts; eyes commonly red but in southeastern U.S. may be white or orange. *Female:* brown "hood" and upperparts.
Size: *L* 7–8½ in; *W* 10½ in.
Voice: song is 2 high, whistled notes followed by a trill: *drink your teeeee;* call is a scratchy, slurred *cheweee!* or *chewink!*
Status: common permanent resident; becoming less common in mountains in winter.
Habitat: along woodland edges, in shrubby, abandoned fields and residential areas.

Similar Birds

Dark-eyed Junco
(p. 166)

Look For

Showy towhees are easily attracted to feeders, where they scratch on the ground for millet, oats or sunflower seeds.

black back, "hood" and bill

rufous sides and flanks

♂

small, white wing patch

♀

Nesting: on the ground or low in a dense shrub; female builds a cup nest of twigs, bark strips, grass and animal hair; pale, brown-spotted eggs are ⅞ x ⅝ in; mainly the female incubates 3–4 eggs for 12–13 days.

Did You Know?

The Eastern Towhee and its similar western relative, the Spotted Towhee (*P. maculatus*), were grouped together as a single species called "Rufous-sided Towhee" until 1995.

Song Sparrow
Melospiza melodia

The well-named Song Sparrow is among the great singers of the bird world. When a young male Song Sparrow is only a few months old, he has already created a courtship tune of his own, having learned the basics of melody and rhythm from his father and rival males. • In winter, adaptable Song Sparrows are common throughout North Carolina and inhabit woodland edges, weedy ditches and riparian thickets. They regularly visit backyard feeders, belting out their sweet, three-part song throughout the year.

Other ID: brown line behind eye; mottled brown upperparts; rounded tail tip.
Size: *L* 6–7 in; *W* 8 in.
Voice: song is 1–4 introductory notes, such as *sweet sweet sweet,* followed by buzzy *towee,* then a short, descending trill; call is short *tsip* or *tchep.*
Status: common permanent resident statewide but breeds from the mountains to the Piedmont farther east in the northern part of the state, including the upper Outer Banks.
Habitat: willow shrub lands, riparian thickets, forest openings and pastures, all often near water.

Similar Birds

Fox Sparrow

Swamp Sparrow

Savannah Sparrow

white jaw line with dark "mustache" stripe

dark crown with pale central stripe

grayish face

heavy brown streaks converge at central breast spot

Nesting: usually on the ground or in a low shrub; female builds an open cup nest of grass, weeds and bark strips; brown-blotched, greenish white eggs are ⅞ x ⅝ in; female incubates 3–5 eggs for 12–14 days.

Did You Know?

Song Sparrows did not breed in North Carolina until the 1930s.

Look For

The Song Sparrow pumps its long, rounded tail in flight. It also often issues a high-pitched *seet* flight call.

White-throated Sparrow

Zonotrichia albicollis

The White-throated Sparrow belts out a distinctive melody year-round, making it one of the easiest sparrows to identify. Its familiar, bold, white throat and striped crown may be confused only with the White-crowned Sparrow (*Z. leucophrys*), but the two birds favor different habitats. White-throats usually stick to forested woodlands, whereas White-crowns prefer open, bushy habitats and farmlands. • Two color morphs are common: one has black and white stripes on the head; the other has brown and tan stripes.

Other ID: gray "cheek"; black eye line; mottled brown upperparts.
Size: L 6½–7½ in; W 9 in.
Voice: variable song is a clear, distinct, whistled: *Old Sam Peabody, Peabody, Peabody;* call is a sharp *chink*.
Status: common winter resident.
Habitat: woodlots, wooded parks and riparian brush.

Similar Birds

White-crowned
Sparrow

Swamp Sparrow

black and white
(or brown and tan)
stripes on head

yellow lores

grayish
bill

white
throat

white-striped morph

Nesting: does not nest in North Carolina; nests in the northeastern U.S. and in Canada; on or near the ground, often concealed by a low shrub or fallen log; open cup nest of plant material is lined with fine grass and hair; variably marked, bluish eggs are $7/8$ x $9/16$ in; female incubates 4–5 eggs for 11–14 days.

Did You Know?

Zonotrichia means "hair-like," a reference to the striped heads of birds in this genus.

Look For

Urban backyards dressed with brushy fenceline tangles and a bird feeder brimming with seeds can attract good numbers of these delightful sparrows in winter.

Dark-eyed Junco

Junco hyemalis

Dark-eyed Juncos usually congregate in backyards with bird feeders and sheltering conifers—with such amenities at their disposal, more and more juncos are appearing in urban areas. These birds spend most of their time on the ground, snatching up seeds underneath bird feeders, and they are readily flushed from wooded trails and backyard feeders. Their distinctive, white outer tail feathers flash in alarm as they seek cover in a nearby tree or shrub. • Look for juncos along the Blue Ridge Parkway, in Great Smoky Mountains NP and on Grandfather Mountain.

Other ID: *Female:* gray-brown where male is slate gray.
Size: L 6–7 in; W 9 in.
Voice: song is a long, dry trill; call is a smacking *chip* note, often given in series.
Status: common permanent resident in the mountains; migrant and winter resident in the rest of the state.
Habitat: shrubby woodland borders and backyard feeders.

Similar Birds

Eastern Towhee
(p. 160)

Look For

This bird will flash its distinctive white outer tail feathers as it rushes for cover after being flushed.

pale pink bill

dark slate
gray overall

white outer
tail feathers

white belly
and undertail
coverts

"Slate-colored Junco"

Nesting: usually above 3500 ft elevation; on the
ground, usually concealed; female builds a cup
nest of twigs, grass, bark shreds and moss;
brown-marked, whitish to bluish eggs are ¾ x ½ in;
female incubates 3–5 eggs for 12–13 days.

Did You Know?

There are five closely related Dark-eyed Junco subspecies
in North America that share similar habits but differ in
coloration and range. The "Slate-colored Junco" is the
subspecies that is widespread and common in eastern
North America.

Northern Cardinal
Cardinalis cardinalis

A male Northern Cardinal will display his unforgettable, vibrant red head crest and raise his tail when he is excited or agitated. This colorful, year-round resident will vigorously defend his territory, even attacking his own reflection in a window or hubcap! • Cardinals are one of only a few bird species to maintain strong pair bonds. Some couples sing to each other year-round, while others join loose flocks, reestablishing pair bonds in spring during a "courtship feeding." A male offers a seed to the female, which she then accepts and eats. • The cardinal is the state bird of North Carolina.

Other ID: *Male:* red overall. *Female:* brownish buff overall; fainter "mask"; red crest, wings and tail.
Size: *L* 8–9 in; *W* 12 in.
Voice: call is a metallic *chip;* song is series of clear, bubbly whistled notes: *What cheer! What cheer! birdie-birdie-birdie what cheer!*
Status: common permanent resident.
Habitat: brushy thickets and shrubby tangles along forest and woodland edges; backyards and urban and suburban parks.

Similar Birds

Summer Tanager

Scarlet Tanager
(p. 158)

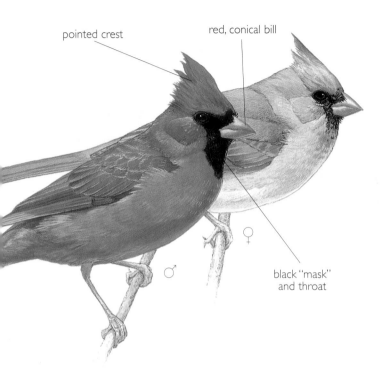

pointed crest

red, conical bill

black "mask" and throat

♂

♀

Nesting: in a dense shrub, vine tangle or low in a coniferous tree; female builds an open cup nest of twigs, grass and bark shreds; brown-blotched, white to greenish white eggs are 1 x ¾ in; female incubates 3–4 eggs for 12–13 days.

Did You Know?

This bird owes its name to the vivid red plumage of the male, which resembles the robes of Roman Catholic cardinals.

Look For

Northern Cardinals fly with jerky movements and short glides and have a preference for sunflower seeds.

Rose-breasted Grosbeak
Pheucticus ludovicianus

Rose-breasted Grosbeaks breed commonly in the Appalachians and occasionally in the Piedmont, usually building their nests low in a tree or tall shrub. By contrast, they typically forage high in the canopy where they can be difficult to spot. Luckily for birders, the abundance of berries in fall often draws these birds to ground level, and they regularly visit feeders stocked with sunflowers during spring migration. Look for this bird at Blue Ridge Parkway, Mount Mitchell SP and Grandfather Mountain.

Other ID: dark tail. *Male:* red breast and inner underwings; white underparts and rump. *Female:* thin crown stripe; brown upperparts; buff underparts with dark brown streaking.
Size: *L* 7–8½ in; *W* 12½ in.
Voice: song is a long, melodious series of whistled notes, much like a fast version of a robin's song; call is a distinctive squeak.
Status: common summer resident in the mountains and common migrant; uncommon to fairly common migrant elsewhere.
Habitat: deciduous and mixed forests.

Similar Birds

Blue Grosbeak

Purple Finch

bold, whitish "eyebrow"

dark wings with
small white patches

black "hood"
and back

pale, conical bill

♀ breeding

♂

Nesting: fairly low in a tree or tall shrub, often near water; mostly the female builds a flimsy cup nest of plant material, lined with rootlets and hair; greenish blue, spotted eggs are 1 x ¹¹⁄₁₆ in; pair incubates 3–5 eggs for 13–14 days.

Did You Know?

In French, *gros bec* means "large beak," and grosbeak bills are well-adapted to the task of crushing seeds, a principal food source for these birds.

Look For

These birds are sometimes confused with sparrows, but grosbeaks have large bills whereas sparrows have small, conical bills.

Indigo Bunting
Passerina cyanea

The vivid electric blue male Indigo Bunting is one of the most spectacular birds in North Carolina. He is a persistent singer, vocalizing even through the heat of a summer day. • These birds arrive in April or May and favor blackberry patches as nest sites. Dense, thorny stems keep most predators at a distance, and the berries are a good food source. • You may find Indigo Buntings at overlooks on the Blue Ridge Parkway, agricultural fields in the Piedmont and in open, shrubby habitats in the Coastal Plain.

Other ID: beady black eyes; black legs; no wing bars. *Male:* bright blue overall; black lores. *Female:* soft brown overall; whitish throat.
Size: L 5½ in; W 8 in.
Voice: song consists of paired warbled whistles: *fire-fire, where-where, here-here, see-it see-it;* call is a quick *spit.*
Status: common summer resident and migrant statewide.
Habitat: deciduous forest and woodland edges, regenerating forest clearings, orchards and shrubby fields.

Similar Birds

Blue Grosbeak

Eastern Bluebird
(p. 138)

darker blue head

gray, conical bill

♂

♀

faint brown streaks
on breast

wings and tail
may show
some black

breeding

Nesting: in a small tree, shrub or within a vine
tangle; female builds a cup nest of grass, leaves
and bark strips; unmarked, white to bluish white
eggs are ¾ x ½ in; female incubates 3–4 eggs for
12–13 days.

Did You Know?

Females choose the most
melodious males as
mates, because these
males can usually estab-
lish territories with the
finest habitat.

Look For

The Indigo Bunting will land
midway on a stem of grass
or a weed and shuffle slowly
toward the seed head, bend-
ing down the stem to reach
the seeds.

Red-winged Blackbird
Agelaius phoeniceus

The male Red-winged Blackbird wears his bright red shoulders like armor—together with his short, raspy song, they are key in defending his territory from rivals. In field experiments, males whose red shoulders were painted black soon lost their territories. • Nearly every cattail marsh in North Carolina plays host to Red-winged Blackbirds during at least some of the year. In winter, look for this species at Pocosin Lakes NWR, Alligator River NWR and Lake Mattamuskeet NWR.

Other ID: *Male:* black overall.
Size: *L* 7½–9 in; *W* 13 in.
Voice: song is a loud, raspy *konk-a-ree* or *ogle-reeeee;* calls include a harsh *check* and high *tseert;* female gives a loud *che-che-che chee chee chee.*
Status: common permanent resident; abundant in winter at the coast; uncommon in the mountains in winter.
Habitat: cattail marshes, wet meadows and ditches, croplands and shoreline shrubs.

Similar Birds

Rusty Blackbird

Brown-headed Cowbird (p. 178)

faint, red shoulder patch on mottled brown upperparts

pale eyebrow

♂

red shoulder patch edged in yellow

♀

heavily streaked underparts

Nesting: colonial; in cattails or shoreline bushes; female builds an open cup nest of dried cattail leaves, lined with fine grass; darkly marked, pale bluish green eggs are 1 x ¾ in; female incubates 3–4 eggs for 10–12 days.

Did You Know?

Some scientists believe that the Red-winged Blackbird is the most abundant bird species in North America.

Look For

Red-winged Blackbirds gather in immense flocks in agricultural areas and open fields in winter.

Eastern Meadowlark
Sturnella magna

The drab dress of most female songbirds lends them and their nestlings protection during the breeding season, but the female Eastern Meadowlark uses a different strategy. Her "V" "necklace" and bright yellow throat and belly create a colorful distraction to lead predators away from the nest. A female flushed from the nest while incubating her eggs will often abandon the nest, and though she will never abandon her chicks, her extra vigilance following a threat usually results in less frequent feeding of nestlings.

Other ID: blackish crown stripes and eye line border; pale "eyebrow" and median crown stripe; dark streaking on white sides and flanks.

Size: *L* 9–9½ in; *W* 14 in.

Voice: song is a rich series of 2–8 melodic, clear, slurred whistles: *see-you at school-today* or *this is the year;* gives a rattling flight call and a high, buzzy *dzeart.*

Status: common permanent resident; more common at the coast in winter; less common in the mountains in winter.

Habitat: grassy meadows and pastures, some croplands, weedy fields, grassy roadsides and old orchards; also coastal barrens in migration and winter.

Similar Birds

Dickcissel

Look For

The Eastern Meadowlark often whistles its proud song from fence posts and power lines.

white jaw line

yellow lores

long, sharp bill

short, wide tail with white outer tail feathers

broad, black breastband

breeding

Nesting: in a concealed depression on the ground; female builds a domed grass nest woven into surrounding vegetation; heavily spotted, white eggs are 1⅛ x ¾ in; female incubates 3–7 eggs for 13–15 days.

Did You Know?

The name suggests that this bird is a lark, but it is actually a brightly colored member of the blackbird family. Its silhouette reveals its blackbird features.

Brown-headed Cowbird
Molothrus ater

These nomads historically followed bison herds across the Great Plains (they now follow cattle), so they never stayed in one area long enough to build and tend a nest. Instead, cowbirds lay their eggs in other birds' nests, relying on the unsuspecting adoptive parents to incubate the eggs and feed the aggressive young. Orioles, warblers, vireos and tanagers are among the most affected species. Increased livestock farming and fragmentation of forests has encouraged the expansion of the cowbird's range and it now parasitizes more than 140 bird species.

Other ID: thick, conical bill; short, squared tail.
Size: *L* 6–8 in; *W* 12 in.
Voice: song is a high, liquidy gurgle: *glug-ahl-whee* or *bubbloozeee;* call is a squeaky, high-pitched *seep, psee* or *wee-tse-tse* or a fast, chipping *ch-ch-ch-ch-ch-ch.*
Status: common permanent resident statewide; more abundant in the Coastal Plain, especially in winter.
Habitat: agricultural and residential areas.

Similar Birds

Rusty Blackbird

Common Grackle

dark eyes

pale throat

dark brown head

light brown underparts with faint streaking

♀

iridescent, green-blue body plumage looks glossy black

♂

Nesting: does not build a nest; female lays up to 40 eggs a year in the nests of other birds, usually 1 egg per nest; brown-speckled, whitish eggs are $7/8 \times 5/8$ in; eggs hatch after 10–13 days.

Did You Know?

When courting a female, the male cowbird points his bill upward to the sky, fans his tail and wings and utters a loud *squeek*.

Look For

When cowbirds feed in flocks, they hold their back ends up high, with their tails sticking straight up in the air.

Orchard Oriole
Icterus spurius

Orchards may once have been favored haunts of this oriole, but because orchards are now heavily sprayed and manicured, it is unlikely that you will ever see this bird in such a locale. Instead, the Orchard Oriole is most commonly found in large shade trees that line roads, paths and streams. Smaller than all other North American orioles, the Orchard Oriole is one of only two oriole species commonly found in the eastern United States. • These orioles are frequent victims of nest parasitism by Brown-headed Cowbirds. In some parts of their breeding range, over half of the nests are parasitized by cowbirds.

Other ID: *Female* and *immature:* olive upperparts; yellow to olive yellow underparts; faint, white wing bars on dusky gray wings.
Size: *L* 6–7 in; *W* 9½ in.
Voice: song is a loud, rapid, varied series of whistled notes; call is a quick *chuck*.
Status: common summer resident statewide; rare above 3000 ft in the mountains.
Habitat: open woodlands, suburban parklands, forest edges, hedgerows and groves of shade trees.

Similar Birds

Baltimore Oriole

Summer Tanager

Scarlet Tanager
(p. 158)

black "hood"

dark wings with
white wing bar and
feather edgings

♀

♂

chestnut underparts,
shoulder and rump

Nesting: in a fork of a deciduous tree or shrub;
female builds a hanging pouch nest woven from
grass and plant fibers; pale bluish white, blotched
eggs are ¾ x ⁹⁄₁₆ in; female incubates 4–5 eggs for
about 12–15 days.

Did You Know?

The Orchard Oriole is
one of the first species to
migrate following breed-
ing and is usually absent
by the beginning of
August.

Look For

Orchard Orioles are best
seen in spring when eager
males hop from branch to
branch, singing their quick
and musical courtship songs.

House Finch
Carpodacus mexicanus

A native to western North America, the House Finch was brought to eastern parts of the continent as an illegally captured cage bird known as the "Hollywood Finch." In the early 1940s, New York pet shop owners released their birds to avoid prosecution and fines, and it is the descendants of those birds that have colonized our area. In fact, the House Finch is now commonly found throughout the continental United States and southern Canada and has been introduced to Hawaii. • Only the resourceful House Finch has been aggressive and stubborn enough to successfully outcompete the House Sparrow.

Other ID: streaked undertail coverts. *Female:* indistinct facial patterning; heavily streaked underparts.
Size: *L* 5–6 in; *W* 9½ in.
Voice: song is a bright, disjointed warble lasting about 3 seconds, often ending with a harsh *jeeer* or *wheer;* flight call is a sweet *cheer,* given singly or in series.
Status: common permanent resident statewide.
Habitat: cities, towns and agricultural areas.

Similar Birds

Purple Finch

Red Crossbill

short bill with curved tip

brown-streaked back

heavily streaked flanks

bright red "eyebrow," forecrown, throat and breast

♀

♂

square tail

Nesting: in a cavity, building, dense foliage or an abandoned bird nest; open cup nest is made of plants and other debris; pale blue, spotted eggs are ¾ x ⁹⁄₁₆ in; female incubates 4–5 eggs for 12–14 days.

Did You Know?

The male House Finch's plumage varies in color from light yellow to bright red, but females choose the reddest males with which to breed.

Look For

In flight, the House Finch has a square tail; the similar-looking Purple Finch has a sharply notched tail.

Glossary

accipiter: a forest hawk (genus *Accipiter*); characterized by a long tail and short, rounded wings; feeds mostly on birds.

brood: *n.* a family of young from one hatching; *v.* to sit on eggs so as to hatch them.

buteo: a high-soaring hawk (genus *Buteo*); characterized by broad wings and short, wide tails; feeds mostly on small mammals and other land animals.

cere: a fleshy area at the base of a bird's bill that contains the nostrils.

clutch: the number of eggs laid by the female at one time.

corvid: a member of the crow family (Corvidae); includes crows, jays, ravens and magpies.

covey: a group of birds, usually grouse or quail.

crop: an enlargement of the esophagus; serves as a storage structure and (in pigeons) has glands that produce secretions.

dabbling: a foraging technique used by ducks, in which the head and neck are submerged but the body and tail remain on the water's surface; dabbling ducks can usually walk easily on land, can take off without running and have brightly colored speculums.

eclipse plumage: a cryptic plumage, similar to that of females, worn by some male ducks in fall when they molt their flight feathers and consequently are unable to fly.

fledgling: a young bird that has left the nest but is dependent upon its parents.

flushing: a behavior in which frightened birds explode into flight in response to a disturbance.

flycatching: a feeding behavior in which the bird leaves a perch, snatches an insect in midair and returns to the same perch.

hawking: attempting to catch insects through aerial pursuit.

irruptive: when a bird is abundant in some years and almost absent in others.

leading edge: the front edge of the wing as viewed from below.

mantle: feathers of the back and upperside of folded wings.

morph: one of several alternate plumages displayed by members of a species.

niche: an ecological role filled by a species.

nocturnal: active during the night.

pelagic: open ocean habitat very far from land.

polyandry: a mating strategy in which one female breeds with several males.

precocial: a bird that is relatively well developed at hatching; precocial birds usually have open eyes, extensive down and are fairly mobile.

primaries: the outermost flight feathers.

raptor: a carnivorous (meat-eating) bird; includes eagles, hawks, falcons and owls.

riparian: refers to habitat along riverbanks.

rufous: rusty red in color.

sexual dimorphism: a difference in plumage, size or other characteristics between males and females of the same species.

speculum: a brightly colored patch on the wings of many dabbling ducks.

stoop: a steep dive through the air, usually performed by birds of prey while foraging or during courtship displays.

Checklist

The following checklist contains 379 species of birds that have been officially recorded as regular in North Carolina. Species are grouped by family and listed in taxonomic order in accordance with the A.O.U. *Check-list of North American Birds* (7th ed.) and its supplements. In addition, the following risk categories are also noted: endangered (en) and threatened (th).

We wish to thank the Carolina Bird Club for their kind assistance in providing the information for this checklist.

Waterfowl
- ❏ Fulvous Whistling-Duck
- ❏ Greater White-fronted Goose
- ❏ Snow Goose
- ❏ Ross's Goose
- ❏ Brant
- ❏ Canada Goose
- ❏ Mute Swan
- ❏ Tundra Swan
- ❏ Wood Duck
- ❏ Gadwall
- ❏ Eurasian Wigeon
- ❏ American Wigeon
- ❏ American Black Duck
- ❏ Mallard
- ❏ Blue-winged Teal
- ❏ Cinnamon Teal
- ❏ Northern Shoveler
- ❏ Northern Pintail
- ❏ Green-winged Teal
- ❏ Canvasback
- ❏ Redhead
- ❏ Ring-necked Duck
- ❏ Greater Scaup
- ❏ Lesser Scaup
- ❏ King Eider
- ❏ Common Eider
- ❏ Harlequin Duck
- ❏ Surf Scoter
- ❏ White-winged Scoter
- ❏ Black Scoter
- ❏ Long-tailed Duck
- ❏ Bufflehead
- ❏ Common Goldeneye
- ❏ Hooded Merganser
- ❏ Common Merganser
- ❏ Red-breasted Merganser
- ❏ Ruddy Duck

Grouse & Allies
- ❏ Ring-necked Pheasant
- ❏ Ruffed Grouse
- ❏ Wild Turkey

New World Quails
- ❏ Northern Bobwhite

Loons
- ❏ Red-throated Loon
- ❏ Pacific Loon
- ❏ Common Loon

Grebes
- ❏ Pied-billed Grebe
- ❏ Horned Grebe
- ❏ Red-necked Grebe
- ❏ Eared Grebe
- ❏ Western Grebe

Petrels & Shearwaters
- ❏ Northern Fulmar
- ❏ Herald Petrel
- ❏ Burmuda Petrel
- ❏ Black-capped Petrel
- ❏ Fea's Petrel
- ❏ Cory's Shearwater
- ❏ Greater Shearwater
- ❏ Sooty Shearwater
- ❏ Manx Shearwater
- ❏ Audubon's Shearwater

Storm-Petrels
- ❏ Wilson's Storm-Petrel
- ❏ White-faced Storm-Petrel
- ❏ Leach's Storm-Petrel
- ❏ Band-rumped Storm-Petrel

Tropicbirds
- ❏ White-tailed Tropicbird
- ❏ Red-billed Tropicbird

Boobies & Gannets
- ❏ Masked Booby
- ❏ Brown Booby
- ❏ Northern Gannet

Pelicans
- ❏ American White Pelican
- ❏ Brown Pelican

Cormorants
- ❏ Double-crested Cormorant
- ❏ Great Cormorant

Darters
- ❏ Anhinga

Frigatebirds
- ❏ Magnificent Frigatebird

Herons
- ❏ American Bittern
- ❏ Least Bittern
- ❏ Great Blue Heron
- ❏ Great Egret
- ❏ Snowy Egret
- ❏ Little Blue Heron
- ❏ Tricolored Heron
- ❏ Reddish Egret
- ❏ Cattle Egret
- ❏ Green Heron
- ❏ Black-crowned Night-Heron
- ❏ Yellow-crowned Night-Heron

Ibises & Spoonbills
- ❏ White Ibis
- ❏ Glossy Ibis
- ❏ Roseate Spoonbill

Storks
- ❏ Wood Stork (en)

Vultures
- ❏ Black Vulture
- ❏ Turkey Vulture

Kites, Hawks & Eagles
- ❏ Osprey
- ❏ Swallow-tailed Kite
- ❏ Mississippi Kite
- ❏ Bald Eagle (th)
- ❏ Northern Harrier
- ❏ Sharp-shinned Hawk
- ❏ Cooper's Hawk
- ❏ Northern Goshawk
- ❏ Red-shouldered Hawk
- ❏ Broad-winged Hawk
- ❏ Red-tailed Hawk
- ❏ Rough-legged Hawk
- ❏ Golden Eagle

Falcons
- ❏ American Kestrel
- ❏ Merlin
- ❏ Peregrine Falcon

Rails & Coots
- ❏ Yellow Rail
- ❏ Black Rail
- ❏ Clapper Rail
- ❏ King Rail
- ❏ Virginia Rail
- ❏ Sora
- ❏ Purple Gallinule
- ❏ Common Moorhen
- ❏ American Coot

Cranes
- ❏ Sandhill Crane

Plovers
- ❏ Black-bellied Plover
- ❏ American Golden-Plover
- ❏ Wilson's Plover
- ❏ Semipalmated Plover
- ❏ Piping Plover (th)
- ❏ Killdeer

Oystercatchers
- ❏ American Oystercatcher

Stilts & Avocets
- ❏ Black-necked Stilt
- ❏ American Avocet

Sandpipers & Allies
- ❏ Greater Yellowlegs
- ❏ Lesser Yellowlegs
- ❏ Solitary Sandpiper
- ❏ Willet
- ❏ Spotted Sandpiper
- ❏ Upland Sandpiper
- ❏ Whimbrel
- ❏ Long-billed Curlew
- ❏ Hudsonian Godwit

❑ Marbled Godwit
❑ Ruddy Turnstone
❑ Red Knot
❑ Sanderling
❑ Semipalmated Sandpiper
❑ Western Sandpiper
❑ Least Sandpiper
❑ White-rumped Sandpiper
❑ Baird's Sandpiper
❑ Pectoral Sandpiper
❑ Purple Sandpiper
❑ Dunlin
❑ Curlew Sandpiper
❑ Stilt Sandpiper
❑ Buff-breasted Sandpiper
❑ Ruff
❑ Short-billed Dowitcher
❑ Long-billed Dowitcher
❑ Wilson's Snipe
❑ American Woodcock
❑ Wilson's Phalarope
❑ Red-necked Phalarope
❑ Red Phalarope

Gulls & Allies
❑ Great Skua
❑ South Polar Skua
❑ Pomarine Jaeger
❑ Parasitic Jaeger
❑ Long-tailed Jaeger
❑ Laughing Gull
❑ Franklin's Gull
❑ Little Gull
❑ Black-headed Gull
❑ Bonaparte's Gull
❑ Ring-billed Gull
❑ California Gull
❑ Herring Gull
❑ Thayer's Gull
❑ Iceland Gull
❑ Lesser Black-backed Gull
❑ Glaucous Gull
❑ Great Black-backed Gull
❑ Sabine's Gull
❑ Black-legged Kittiwake
❑ Gull-billed Tern
❑ Caspian Tern
❑ Royal Tern
❑ Sandwich Tern

❑ Roseate Tern (en)
❑ Common Tern
❑ Arctic Tern
❑ Forster's Tern
❑ Least Tern
❑ Bridled Tern
❑ Sooty Tern
❑ Black Tern
❑ Brown Noddy
❑ Black Skimmer

Alcids
❑ Dovekie
❑ Razorbill

Pigeons & Doves
❑ Rock Pigeon
❑ Eurasian Collared-Dove
❑ White-winged Dove
❑ Mourning Dove
❑ Common Ground-Dove

Cuckoos
❑ Black-billed Cuckoo
❑ Yellow-billed Cuckoo

Barn Owls
❑ Barn Owl

Owls
❑ Eastern Screech-Owl
❑ Great Horned Owl
❑ Snowy Owl
❑ Barred Owl
❑ Long-eared Owl
❑ Short-eared Owl
❑ Northern Saw-whet Owl

Nightjars
❑ Common Nighthawk
❑ Chuck-will's-widow
❑ Whip-poor-will

Swifts
❑ Chimney Swift

Hummingbirds
❑ Ruby-throated Hummingbird
❑ Black-chinned Hummingbird
❑ Rufous Hummingbird

Kingfishers
❑ Belted Kingfisher

Woodpeckers
- ❏ Red-headed Woodpecker
- ❏ Red-bellied Woodpecker
- ❏ Yellow-bellied Sapsucker
- ❏ Downy Woodpecker
- ❏ Hairy Woodpecker
- ❏ Red-cockaded Woodpecker (en)
- ❏ Northern Flicker
- ❏ Pileated Woodpecker

Flycatchers
- ❏ Olive-sided Flycatcher
- ❏ Eastern Wood-Pewee
- ❏ Yellow-bellied Flycatcher
- ❏ Acadian Flycatcher
- ❏ Alder Flycatcher
- ❏ Willow Flycatcher
- ❏ Least Flycatcher
- ❏ Eastern Phoebe
- ❏ Great Crested Flycatcher
- ❏ Western Kingbird
- ❏ Eastern Kingbird
- ❏ Gray Kingbird
- ❏ Scissor-tailed Flycatcher

Shrikes
- ❏ Loggerhead Shrike

Vireos
- ❏ White-eyed Vireo
- ❏ Yellow-throated Vireo
- ❏ Blue-headed Vireo
- ❏ Warbling Vireo
- ❏ Philadelphia Vireo
- ❏ Red-eyed Vireo

Jays & Crows
- ❏ Blue Jay
- ❏ American Crow
- ❏ Fish Crow
- ❏ Common Raven

Larks
- ❏ Horned Lark

Swallows
- ❏ Purple Martin
- ❏ Tree Swallow
- ❏ Northern Rough-winged Swallow
- ❏ Bank Swallow
- ❏ Cliff Swallow
- ❏ Cave Swallow
- ❏ Barn Swallow

Chickadees & Titmice
- ❏ Carolina Chickadee
- ❏ Black-capped Chickadee
- ❏ Tufted Titmouse

Nuthatches
- ❏ Red-breasted Nuthatch
- ❏ White-breasted Nuthatch
- ❏ Brown-headed Nuthatch

Creepers
- ❏ Brown Creeper

Wrens
- ❏ Carolina Wren
- ❏ Bewick's Wren
- ❏ House Wren
- ❏ Winter Wren
- ❏ Sedge Wren
- ❏ Marsh Wren

Kinglets
- ❏ Golden-crowned Kinglet
- ❏ Ruby-crowned Kinglet

Gnatcatchers
- ❏ Blue-gray Gnatcatcher

Thrushes
- ❏ Eastern Bluebird
- ❏ Veery
- ❏ Gray-cheeked Thrush
- ❏ Swainson's Thrush
- ❏ Hermit Thrush
- ❏ Wood Thrush
- ❏ American Robin

Mockingbirds & Thrashers
- ❏ Gray Catbird
- ❏ Northern Mockingbird
- ❏ Brown Thrasher

Starlings
- ❏ European Starling

Pipits
- ❏ American Pipit

Waxwings
- ❏ Cedar Waxwing

Wood-Warblers
- ❏ Blue-winged Warbler
- ❏ Golden-winged Warbler
- ❏ Tennessee Warbler
- ❏ Orange-crowned Warbler

- ❏ Nashville Warbler
- ❏ Northern Parula
- ❏ Yellow Warbler
- ❏ Chestnut-sided Warbler
- ❏ Magnolia Warbler
- ❏ Cape May Warbler
- ❏ Black-throated Blue Warbler
- ❏ Yellow-rumped Warbler
- ❏ Black-throated Green Warbler
- ❏ Blackburnian Warbler
- ❏ Yellow-throated Warbler
- ❏ Pine Warbler
- ❏ Prairie Warbler
- ❏ Palm Warbler
- ❏ Bay-breasted Warbler
- ❏ Blackpoll Warbler
- ❏ Cerulean Warbler
- ❏ Black-and-white Warbler
- ❏ American Redstart
- ❏ Prothonotary Warbler
- ❏ Worm-eating Warbler
- ❏ Swainson's Warbler
- ❏ Ovenbird
- ❏ Northern Waterthrush
- ❏ Louisiana Waterthrush
- ❏ Kentucky Warbler
- ❏ Connecticut Warbler
- ❏ Mourning Warbler
- ❏ Common Yellowthroat
- ❏ Hooded Warbler
- ❏ Wilson's Warbler
- ❏ Canada Warbler
- ❏ Yellow-breasted Chat

Tanagers
- ❏ Summer Tanager
- ❏ Scarlet Tanager
- ❏ Western Tanager

Sparrows & Allies
- ❏ Eastern Towhee
- ❏ Bachman's Sparrow
- ❏ American Tree Sparrow
- ❏ Chipping Sparrow
- ❏ Clay-colored Sparrow
- ❏ Field Sparrow
- ❏ Vesper Sparrow
- ❏ Lark Sparrow
- ❏ Savannah Sparrow
- ❏ Grasshopper Sparrow
- ❏ Henslow's Sparrow
- ❏ Le Conte's Sparrow
- ❏ Nelson's Sharp-tailed Sparrow
- ❏ Saltmarsh Sharp-tailed Sparrow
- ❏ Seaside Sparrow
- ❏ Fox Sparrow
- ❏ Song Sparrow
- ❏ Lincoln's Sparrow
- ❏ Swamp Sparrow
- ❏ White-throated Sparrow
- ❏ White-crowned Sparrow
- ❏ Dark-eyed Junco
- ❏ Lapland Longspur
- ❏ Snow Bunting

Grosbeaks & Buntings
- ❏ Northern Cardinal
- ❏ Rose-breasted Grosbeak
- ❏ Black-headed Grosbeak
- ❏ Blue Grosbeak
- ❏ Indigo Bunting
- ❏ Painted Bunting
- ❏ Dickcissel

Blackbirds & Allies
- ❏ Bobolink
- ❏ Red-winged Blackbird
- ❏ Eastern Meadowlark
- ❏ Yellow-headed Blackbird
- ❏ Rusty Blackbird
- ❏ Brewer's Blackbird
- ❏ Common Grackle
- ❏ Boat-tailed Grackle
- ❏ Shiny Cowbird
- ❏ Brown-headed Cowbird
- ❏ Orchard Oriole
- ❏ Bullock's Oriole
- ❏ Baltimore Oriole

Finches
- ❏ Purple Finch
- ❏ House Finch
- ❏ Red Crossbill
- ❏ White-winged Crossbill
- ❏ Common Redpoll
- ❏ Pine Siskin
- ❏ American Goldfinch
- ❏ Evening Grosbeak

Old World Sparrows
- ❏ House Sparrow

Index